# BRIDGING THE GAP

## Twenty Years After the War
## in Vietnam

## ALSO BY CHARLES D. PILON

ARIZONA GOVERNMENT

ARIZONA GOVERNMENT WORKBOOK

CONSTITUTION OF THE UNITED STATES

# BRIDGING THE GAP

## Twenty Years After the War in Vietnam

## by CHARLES D. PILON

**Foreword by The Honorable John McCain,
United States Senate**

**Quail Publications**
Phoenix, Arizona

**Bridging the Gap:** Twenty Years after the War in Vietnam

Printed and bound in the United States of America


Cover by Ken Reaser / Square One Design
Photographs by the author
Proofread by Ray Newton

Library of Congress Cataloging in Publication Data

Pilon, Charles Damon, 1933-
Bridging the Gap: Twenty Years after the War in Vietnam: foreword by U.S. Senator John McCain.

Includes reading recommendations and index.
1. Vietnam, 1994-Nonfiction        2. Travel Essay

ISBN 1-889052-03-5


I. Title        II. Title: Bridging the gap, twenty years after the war in Vietnam.
III. Title: Bridging the gap, twenty years after the war in Vietnam.

Library of Congress Catalog Card Number: 96-92168

# DEDICATION

I dedicate this book to

Every American man and woman who served with the military in
    Vietnam,

Every American man and woman whose name appears on
    "The Wall" in Washington, D.C.,

Every man and woman who served in Vietnam and died in the
    United States, from wounds both physical and mental,
    whose names do not appear on  "The Wall,"

All the innocent men, women, and children who died in the
    war, just because they were Vietnamese,

All the peace loving people of Vietnam today, who just want
    peace between our nations.

# ACKNOWLEDGEMENTS

My sincere gratitude to:

Roy Morey, for having the insight to realize how richly rewarded I would be from this unique experience, and for his generosity in making the complicated arrangements that were so necessary to complete this mission in Vietnam.

Delores Morey, for her warm and gracious hospitality, and for all the time she spent making sure we saw and did everything possible to really appreciate the Vietnamese and their society. The longtime friendship shared by the Moreys and Pilons, made this trip even more meaningful.

Ray Newton, for his guidance and encouragement in motivating me to complete my manuscript. His knowledge and expertise in proofreading were invaluable.

U.S. Senator John McCain, for making me feel welcome when I visited him in his Phoenix office and for his willingness to write the foreword.

Nguyen Xuan Thuan, for overseeing a rich cultural experience in the southern area of Vietnam, especially Ho Chi Minh City.

My wife Linda, who "bridged the gap" with me in Vietnam, and then typed and edited this manuscript, bringing the project to fruition.

**JOHN McCAIN**
ARIZONA

COMMITTEE ON ARMED SERVICES

COMMITTEE ON COMMERCE, SCIENCE,
AND TRANSPORTATION

COMMITTEE ON GOVERNMENTAL AFFAIRS

COMMITTEE ON INDIAN AFFAIRS

## United States Senate

241 RUSSELL SENATE OFFICE BUILDING
WASHINGTON, DC 20510-0303
(202) 224-2235

1839 SOUTH ALMA SCHOOL ROAD
SUITE 375
MESA, AZ 85210
(602) 491-4300

2400 EAST ARIZONA
BILTMORE CIRCLE
SUITE 1150
PHOENIX, AZ 85016
(602) 952-2410

450 WEST PASEO REDONDO
SUITE 200
TUCSON, AZ 85701
(520) 670-6334

TELEPHONE FOR HEARING IMPAIRED
(202) 224-7132
(602) 952-0170

## FOREWORD

I read with great interest the account of Dr. Pilon's recent trip to Vietnam. His service to the nation in Korea gives him a distinctive and valuable perspective. Like most veterans, he understands that conflicts must come to an end. Our enemies in war do not remain enemies forever. In fact, there comes a day when -- far from the field of battle -- we may count some of them as our friends.

He seems to have made many new friends on his "mission." The visit with the rector of the Viet Bac Teacher Training College was particularly interesting. Given the similar terrain in which their respective institutions are located and the somewhat similar challenges he faces, I am sure Dr. Pilon will value his friendship with the rector for years to come.

Dr. Pilon is to be commended for his efforts. The Vietnamese need just the sort of assistance in educating their people that he can offer. Vietnam is making a great leap from a Socialist economy with no relevance beyond its borders, to what many have proclaimed the next Asian economic tiger. As Dr. Pilon knows from his experience as a teacher, education is central to successfully competing in the world economy. Like the U.S., Vietnam's prosperity depends on its competitiveness, and its competitiveness depends on the proper education of its people.

On a lighter note, Dr. Pilon should also be commended for his patience in dealing with the Vietnamese bureaucracy. My wife, Cindy, and I sympathize with Chuck and Linda. Bureaucracies have rightfully earned the enmity of travellers around the world and Vietnam produces its fair share of very typically frustrating bureaucrats.

It was a joy to read Dr. Pilon's book.

Sincerely,

John McCain
United States Senator

# PREFACE

A rare opportunity was presented to me when Dr. Roy D. Morey, Resident Representative of the United Nations Development Programme in Vietnam, proposed that I, an administrator with Northern Arizona University, make a mission to Vietnam upon the joint request of the UNDP and the Government of Vietnam. Considering the possibilities of these three agencies cooperating and understanding the complete mission, I thought it was probable that much confusion and misunderstanding might occur. Low and behold, all the planning, arranging, and scheduling came together, and the mission was a go. I had no idea what to expect from the Vietnamese government. I was confident that everything from the United Nations Development Programme office in Hanoi would be well managed. I thought Northern Arizona would be eager for me to participate in the project. The red tape started to unravel, then completely disappear by the time my departure date was nearing. From individuals that I see and associate with, family and friends included, I did not receive much encouragement for the trip. For older Americans, the war is still freshly imprinted on their minds, even after two decades. Some individuals predicted that my life would not be safe. Others questioned at great length why I would bother or even want to go to "that" nation where we had fought a war. No one said it, but their looks gave me the impression that just maybe I was being disloyal or not quite patriotic because I was going to Vietnam. I did not receive much encouragement for this mission. They did not understand that I was not going just to see. I was going to become involved and interact with Vietnamese officials, educators, and citizens. This was not a sight-seeing trip. It was to be a mission of peace, understanding, cooperation, and good will. I had complete confidence in myself, first as a human being, second as an educator, and third as an American, to put my best foot forward in all contacts, as I represented American education, Northern Arizona University, the state of Arizona, and the United States of America. I was ready and I did it. It was an incredible journey, a worthwhile mission, and an experience beyond description, until I wrote these words.

Ho Chi Minh City,September 30,1995

Dr. Charles D. Pilon
5711 N. 12 th Place
Phoenix,AZ 8514

Dear Dr. Charles D. Pilon,

Thank you for your MISSION TO VIETNAM sent to us through UNDP,Ha Noi and Ho Chi Minh Open University feels happy and pround to be one of your eleven chapters written in the book.

It is not long time since our last meeting but it is long enough for Ho Chi Minh Open University to achieve enormous developments.The total numbers of students enrolled at present is 38,000.Besides on-campus classes,we have offered Busines Administration in distance learning programmes serving aroung 5,000 students in the Central and the South of Vietnam.Our new Faculty is the Post Graduate Faculty which provides M.B.A. degree and together with Universite Libre de Bruxelles [ Belgium ] delivering  M.M. degree.We plan to build a new 7-stories building on the old site of Ho Chi Minh Open University but still keep the front part where the President's room and the Conference room are situated by the end of the year.

We are happy with the normalization of the relationship between the United States of America and Vietnam and I think that your precious book is one of the brick building the bridge of cooperation and friedship between the two countries. I am looking forward to seeing you again to show you more about Ho Chi Minh Open University.

With my best regards,I remain.
Sincerely yours,

Dr. Cao Van Phuong
President
Ho Chi Minh Open University

For most Americans, the twenty year period after the end of the Viet Nam war, Viet Nam remained a mystery. Travel was difficult, information was lacking. Communications were virtually non-existent. The situation began changing in 1993 and the process of broadening and expanding knowledge and information has accelerated since the establishment of diplomatic relations between the United States and Viet Nam in July 1995.

There were a few Americans who decided to visit Viet Nam, learn something about the country, the people and judge for themselves. Such was the case with Chuck and Linda Pilon of Phoenix, Arizona. We can be grateful that the visit made such a strong impression on Chuck because he decided to record his experience in *Mission to Viet Nam* . Having known Chuck for most of my life, I was not surprised the visit made such an impact because of his personal qualities and professional interests.

Quite rightly, Chuck describes the Vietnamese people as being warm and hospitable. It should also be said that Chuck is a warm and sensitive person who brings out these same qualities in those with whom he interacts. Hence what comes through in his book is a genuine human touch which gives life and vitality to his observations and stories. Chuck is also a former history teacher and now a university educator. These professional qualities are reflected in the book as well. Without his sense of history, it simply would not have been possible for him to get so much out of a relatively brief visit. Like all educators, he is committed to the belief that the acquisition of knowledge is good for people and good for the world. Educators also believe that you learn the most by asking questions. The book reveals that Chuck is truly unabashed about asking questions even when the answer may lead to an embarrassing situation. In fact, it is his inquisitiveness that leads to some of the most humorous and memorable moments in the account of his experiences.

Most travellers argue that the lasting memories of a country are of the people rather than the landscape. Chuck's book reveals that he has learned this lesson well. Since taking up residence in Hanoi in 1992, I have read a steady stream of books and articles on Viet Nam covering everything from macro-economic policy to changes in social attitudes. Though Chuck Pilon is neither a specialist on Viet Nam nor a resident observer, his book broadened my knowledge of the country and the people; it had the added bonus of being a most enjoyable read.

Roy D. Morey
Resident Representative for Viet Nam
United Nations Development Programme

25-29 Phan Boi Chau, Hanoi (Viet Nam). Tel: (84-4) 257495, 254254, 256419, 257318.
Fax: 259267. Tlx: 411417 UNDP VT. E-Mail: fo.vum@undp.org
Ho Chi Minh City Liaison Office: 2 Phung Khac Khoan. Tel: (84-8) 295821,295965. Fax: 231834. Telex: 811269 UNDP VT.

# CONTENTS

# Chapter One

## VISA VICTORY

Aboard United Flight #845 bound for Taipei, Taiwan, and Bangkok, Thailand, Friday, February 11, 1994, I sat with my wife Linda, stunned to realize, I, Chuck Pilon, was on my way to Vietnam! I am the same guy who in 1965 taught and lived by the quotation of Stephen Decatur, naval hero of the War of Tripoli, "Our country in her intercourse with other nations, may she always be right, but our country, right or wrong." This trip; however, was a mission of peace, good will, and help for the educators I would meet with in Hanoi and Ho Chi Minh City. It all came about due to a friendly conversation in a little campground in Telluride, Colorado, in the summer of 1993.

My wife Linda and I had been on our annual summer camping trip with dear friends, Roy and Delores Morey. Every summer for almost two decades, the Pilons and the Moreys spend a couple of weeks camping together, although the Moreys have lived in such distant and exotic places as Bangkok, Thailand; Apia, Samoa; New York City; Beijing, China; and now Hanoi, Vietnam; where Roy is presently the Resident Representative for the United Nations Development Programme in Vietnam. On that particular outing, Roy seriously asked, "Why don't you come to Hanoi?" I merely let the invitation pass as a casual statement of fantasy. However, Roy seriously got my attention when he said, "Chuck, my office is in the process of completing an analysis of the state of education in Vietnam, and I would like an American educator with your particular expertise and background to visit with educators at Vietnamese universities and colleges." Roy might as well have asked me to journey to Cape Kennedy to board the next shuttle to outer space. Vietnam was a land across the wide Pacific Ocean and also a land even farther removed from my interest and philosophy. Our country was once at war with Vietnam. The Vietnamese were the enemy. I had taught students whose fathers had been killed in Vietnam. I had students who died of wounds received in Vietnam. I even had a relative, Alan E. Pilon, who is memorialized on "The Wall" in Washington, D.C. With fellow teacher Aaron Scholar, I had helped organize a campaign in which students wrote 10,000 letters to the troops in Vietnam. We had received a letter from Lt. Col. H. K. Joost of the 173rd Airborne Brigade in Vietnam stating, "On behalf of several thousands of paratroopers of the command, I wish to thank you for your note of confidence in us." We had even received a certificate and letter from General W. C. Westmoreland, Commanding General of the U.S. Armed Forces in Vietnam, thanking Phoenix for supporting the war effort. General Westmoreland wrote, "The many fine actions by Americans everywhere in writing letters and cards of support, in donating blood to U.S. military personnel, in sending gifts to servicemen, and in aiding our civic action program in Vietnam, are to my knowledge, unprecedented and greatly encouraging." I still have the book, VIETNAM PAST AND PRESENT by Thai Van Kiem, given to me in February of 1966, by Warrant Officers Jim Ikerd and John Christensen, from "The Fangs" in Vietnam. These two helicopter pilots visited our school in Phoenix to personally thank the students for all their support on behalf of the fighting men in Vietnam. It was an exciting time for our students to be recognized as these soldiers presented a model of their aircraft plus a model of a typical Vietnamese village home at a full school assembly. As the presentations were made, I had a lump in my throat. I was so proud of my students, my fellow teachers, and of course these honored guests.

Roy reminded me very quickly that the war had been over for nineteen years and the country is unified, peaceful, and calm. He encouragingly stated that it could be a journey of a lifetime, and rewarding far beyond my imagination. I was doubtful how this could come about. Roy said that on his return to Hanoi, he would confer with officials at the Government of Vietnam Ministry of Education and begin having his staff arrange an itinerary that would knock my socks off. I thought Roy had had too many bottles of Corona, as we sat in my little tent trailer planning the next day's outing to the Tom Boy, an abandoned mining community in a high Colorado mountain pass. Roy's father had worked in this particular mine as a young man, so it had great interest for all of us, but especially for Roy and Delores.

Roy assured me that this trip to Vietnam could happen, should happen, and would happen. I said, "Sure, Roy," as I opened another bottle of Corona. I thought, "Yeah, Roy, you used to tell me I might start the next game when we played football at Arizona State College in Flagstaff many years ago." I had been listening to Roy fantasizing since we were teammates in 1955. Delores and Linda were also trying to convince me that this would be a great opportunity. Here we were, four college chums, who had maintained a thirty-eight-year friendship, planning a rendezvous in Vietnam.

Even that night we discussed the possibility as we were walking to the old Opera House movie theater in Telluride, to see a movie, which ironically happened to be INDOCHINE! Viewing this wonderfully historical film about the French occupation in Vietnam helped to whet my curiosity about the proposed trip. The hope that it might come about began to take shape.

In early September I received the following letter from Roy, who had returned to Hanoi.

18 September 1993

Dear Chuck,

The purpose of this letter is to follow-up on our discussions while we were together in August. As I explained to you, the United Nations Development Programme (UNDP) is the leading international organization in Viet Nam which is assisting the country with its reform process. This role is best illustrated by the fact that UNDP and the World Bank have been requested by the Government to co-Chair Viet Nam's first ever international Donor's Conference to be held in Paris on 9-10 November 1993. There have been 24 countries and 12 international organizations invited to this conference.

As part of the overall reform effort, the education system in Viet Nam will undergo considerable change in the next few years. To help structure this process of change, two years ago the Ministry of Education and Training undertook a major strategic review of education. This effort was launched with support by UNDP and technical assistance by UNESCO. The results of the review are starting to emerge and UNDP will continue to be involved. As mentioned to you, the field of continuing education will certainly receive more intensive and systematic attention. Because of your role and involvement in this field, naturally I thought of you as a resource person who could provide valuable and practical experience to the Vietnamese on the one hand and you could gain insights into a rapidly changing country and educational system on the other. Before commenting more specifically on the type of assignment I would like for you to consider, I will start with a few personal observations on what I see as a likely evolving relationship between Viet Nam and the United States.

More than five years ago, the political leaders in this country started instituting a reform process which has had and will continue to have a profound and positive impact within the country and its relations with other countries. For good reason, the Vietnamese have chosen the restructing of the economy as the "lead-horse" in the reform effort. It will be accompanied by public institution and administrative reforms and reform of the legal structure. One of the most fundamental reform policies of Viet Nam is that of opening to the outside world. There is clear recognition that the country's development goals can best be met by strengthening its linkages with other countries in order to enhance the flow of experience and ideas, modern technology, technical and managerial know-how, trade and investment.

Dr. Charles D. Pilon
5711 N. 12th Place
Phoenix, Arizona 85014
U.S.A.

For a variety of reasons, Viet Nam has a genuine interest in having the U.S. trade embargo lifted and normalizing and strengthening relations between the two countries. In my view, within 15 years, the two countries will have strong and friendly relations with millions of people (many of them ethnic Vietnamese), travelling back and forth across the Pacific.

The most significant opportunity for the US to develop linkages with Viet Nam is obviously in the non-governmental or private sector - universities, research institutes, private business and NGOs. There will be a very strong interest on the part of Vietnamese to study in US universities. Moreover, there is a strong interest (in both the North and South) to learn more about the US.

I certainly hope that you and Linda will take us up on our invitation to visit Viet Nam. In conjunction with such a visit I would like for you to spend some time perusing your professional interest which I feel would be to the benefit of NAU, UNDP and Viet Nam. More specifically I would like for you to make a general presentation on continuing education drawing on your NAU experience. I would arrange for this presentation at the Ministry of Education and Training. In addition I would like to set up visits to several teacher training institutions in Hanoi and Ho Chi Minh City (Saigon). If time permits, I would also like for you to exchange ideas with the staff of an education department of one of the more impoverished provinces in the general vicinity of Hanoi or Haiphong.

While I would very much appreciate your undertaking the work I have described above, I regret to inform you that it would not be possible for UNDP to provide financial support for either your airtravel to Viet Nam or related expenses. I do hope the University will be able to help out in this regard. Naturally, my office would make all arrangements and would provide an interpreter and transport here in the country. Moreover Delores and I would be delighted to have you and Linda stay with us at our residence here in Hanoi. If at all possible I would try to travel with you to Ho Chi Minh City, but in any event the UNDP sub-office there would be responsible for making all arrangements.

As you know, I will be out of the country for much of the next two months in connection with the Donor Conference. For this and other reasons, I would suggest that you make a visit to Viet Nam in March. There are no significant local holidays at that time which would interfere with scheduling meetings. Moreover, the weather at that time is warming up but still pleasant.

Once again Chuck it was wonderful being with you and Linda in August including the brief visit we made to the NAU campus. Please let me know your plans so that I can start making arrangements.

Best regards,

Roy D. Morey
Resident Representative

I was still stunned, surprised, but also very excited about the possibility of making such a trip. I thought about the multitude of plans that had to be arranged and how to go about getting them into effect. I would need to receive permission from the university where I am employed in order to secure official business time-off. I submitted a letter with a copy of Roy's letter to Dr. Patsy Reed, Interim President of Northern Arizona University in Flagstaff and second copies to Dr. Patrick Deegan, Dean of Continuing Education, who is my immediate supervisor. I asked only for university time-off to represent Continuing Education of Northern Arizona University in Vietnam. I did state that I would not refuse any financial help that would be offered. Previously, I had requested university time-off and financial help for various conferences, conventions, workshops, and seminars over the span of 16 years that I had been employed by the university. The time was always granted, but the financial help had been rejected. I was surprised and excited to learn that Dr. Reed was fully aware of previous decisions and stated that it was time to assist Chuck on this worthy mission. Dr. Deegan was willing to match any amount that Dr. Reed was granting. The total sum turned out to be $1000. I was grateful for the remuneration, not realizing at the time that the trip would total over $7000.

Linda made many phone calls to airline companies trying to arrange flights with the least expensive fares to Hanoi, only to be told time and again that American carriers couldn't fly to Vietnam. We knew that because of the US trade embargo imposed against

Vietnam, we would have to enter Vietnam from either Hong Kong or Bangkok. Also these two cities had Vietnamese embassies, which afforded us the opportunity to secure Vietnamese visas. We had previously been to Hong Kong, so we chose to fly via Bangkok, an exotic city we had not already visited. All the airline personnel Linda spoke with recommended first of all that we not go to Vietnam, but that if we insisted, we should definitely fly Thai Air. (Both Thai Air and Vietnam Airlines flew in and out of Hanoi and Ho Chi Minh City but on different days.) She finally deduced that United Airlines offered the best round trip fare, ($1166.43 each) from Phoenix to Bangkok, via San Francisco and Taipei. We booked our flight, but that was only part way. We still had to ask Roy and Delores to have their travel agent in Bangkok reserve flights for us to Vietnam. Of course, when the dates were arranged, the departure date from Bangkok to Hanoi was a day when only Vietnam Air flew, so that's the flight that was scheduled for us. We spent a lot of money sending one fax after another to Roy's office to arrange, change, and rearrange plans. Finally, we completed all arrangements to ship out to Vietnam. We hadn't foreseen so much difficulty in securing these reservations. Three years earlier we had traveled to Beijing, China, at the invitation of Roy and UNDP, to lecture at Beijing Normal University. At that time Roy had been the Resident Representative of UNDP in Beijing. We had a relatively easy time in making arrangements, but the United States had maintained diplomatic relations with China since President Nixon's administration. At the time our plans were being made to go to Vietnam, the trade embargo with Vietnam was still in effect and wouldn't be lifted by President Clinton until February 3, 1994, just a few days prior to our visit.

After 16 hours of flying across the Pacific Ocean and losing a day from crossing the international date line, we landed in Taipei, Taiwan, on February 12, at 8:00 P.M. We left the plane as required and wandered around a huge waiting area, surrounded by large windows darkened by nightfall. We could climb a flight of stairs to walk through the airport shopping area, which we did, but all the tourist shops and restaurants were closed. By now we were close to exhaustion, wanted showers, and still had several hours before we would arrive in Bangkok, Thailand for our first night's stay. We were required to take this layover while flight #845 was cleaned. We finally arrived in Bangkok at 1:00 A.M., on February 13, an hour late. After clearing a very efficient customs and security check, we were so grateful to see a driver holding up a placard printed with PILON on it. He quickly brought his BMW around, loaded our bags, and we began the hour-long drive from the airport to our hotel, the Mansion Kempinski in downtown Bangkok.

My first impression of Bangkok began in a negative manner, because I spotted some teenagers stealing several pieces of luggage from the baggage compartment of a bus stopped in a traffic jam. However, I was impressed by the many Buddhist shrines I saw on the way into town. Our driver asked us if we would like something to drink, as we were approaching the downtown area. We looked at

10

each other in dismay, not wanting to stop anywhere but the hotel, at this point. When he explained that he would arrange to have it waiting for us in our hotel room, we were both relieved and pleased. We said we'd love to have two Coca Colas, which he ordered for us on his car phone. Within minutes, we were stepping into the marble floored lobby and were each presented with a welcoming Thai flower arrangement. The night clerk was most gracious and had us registered and shown to our room very quickly. We were so tired, that we couldn't decide if we wanted showers or just to go to bed; however, the bellman insisted on showing us the television, the CD player, the intricate light system, our robes, and presented us with a hotel folder with our names imprinted in gold on the stationary. Our son Terry would have loved these electronic gadgets. The walls of our room were covered with Thai silk, and there were lovely paintings of local life. Opposite the gigantic king-size bed was a loveseat and coffee table. Sure enough, there were two ice-cold Coca Colas, but to our amazement, there were China plates, linen napkins, stainless flatware, plus a tray of exotic Thai fruits, chocolates, and cookies, all decorated with a small orchid. As exhausted as we were, we sat down to enjoy this wonderful welcoming gesture and got our second wind. We felt extremely pampered and certainly slept well that night.

In the morning, we arranged for a driver to take us to attend Mass, at a Catholic church. It was a very warm day, and the church was extremely crowded. Despite the lack of air conditioning, we were very comfortable, due to the large floor-to-ceiling doors every few feet down each side of the church being left open, so there was quite a breeze flowing around us. The main statue of Christ on the altar was large and very Buddha-like in appearance, and completely covered with gold leaf. The Mass was in English, as were the songs, but we were not familiar with them. However, the music was very much in the Thai style and quite melodic. We felt comfortable and welcome, as it was one of the most meaningful masses we'd attended anywhere.

Since we had no transportation back to the hotel, we decided to be adventurous and return by a three wheel open-air taxi, called a tuk tuk. We knew to ask for a price before we climbed aboard. It amounted to about ninety US cents. I'm sure the doorman and lovely Thai lady who greeted us upon our return, wondered about our choice of travel, as we had spent ten US dollars in going to the church. They probably thought we were accustomed to riding in a limousine.

We decided to have lunch in the hotel dining room, where we were served an exquisite chicken, cashew nut, rice dish. The service was impeccable, and we were the only diners.

Because it was Sunday and we were not able to do any business, the hotel arranged a guide and driver to take us to the Grand Palace and the Wat Po for 1250 baht, (over $50 US dollars.) We toured the grounds and some temples of the Grand Palace compound and viewed the Emerald Buddha and the Reclining Buddha, after removing our shoes, and wondering if we would be able to reclaim our own shoes from the hundreds stacked on shelves

12

outside the temple door. There was no claim check. It was a very casual system, and believe it or not, we found our own shoes with no trouble.

We were fascinated with the outer structure of the temples, a mosaic of tiny pieces of colored glass, flowing gracefully upward to majestic spires. Despite the extreme heat, we enjoyed ourselves very much. On our return to the hotel, our guide said that he would take us to a very special place, a gem factory, to actually witness jewelry being designed and manufactured. As soon as I saw the many tour buses in the tiny parking lot, I knew this was your typical tourist detour. We saw two or three workmen at two long workbenches actually doing something to very small pieces of gold. I don't know if they were really creating anything new, but it didn't matter. We were immediately ushered into the showroom, where there were all types of gem stones plus gems set in every type of jewelry imaginable. It was a huge room with display cases of diamonds, rubies, sapphires, emeralds, and pearls. There was everything anyone could desire. I was so happy that Linda has never really cared for expensive gems. I was about to succumb, but Linda was firm in saying, "No." She didn't even want to purchase any Thai silk or cottons in the adjoining gift shop. I don't think we were too popular with our guide or driver, as they didn't earn any commission that afternoon.

Upon our return to the Mansion Kempinski, we headed straight to our luxurious room. Linda was asleep before 7:00 P.M. I tried to watch a movie on TV. Appropriately, it was GOOD

MORNING, VIETNAM in English with Thai sub-titles. I fell asleep before it ended, and we both awoke at 3:00 A.M. and finally got up at 5:00 A.M. and watched the news on CNN.

We had many travel plans to complete, so it was good we didn't sleep in. Our first stop was at the neighboring Ambassador Hotel for breakfast. The papaya, pineapple, and croissants were superb. From there we hustled to the Moreys' travel agent, Amtra, only a few blocks away. On the way we were constantly barraged by street vendors, who took over most of the sidewalk displaying their wares. Each were selling an assortment of brightly colored t-shirts, carved wooden bowls, lacquered boxes, small animal figurines, overlay embroidered clothing and linens, straw hats, umbrellas, knives, and sunglasses. The competition for our business was intense, and we made excuses not to buy anything, just to be able to move along the sidewalk. Scattered among the stands were various food carts, where fresh papaya, mango, guava, bananas, watermelon, and coconuts were sold. Also many exotic-looking Asian fruits looked tempting. The odors of sizzling poultry or pork, and perhaps even beef were enticing, but we resisted, as it was too early for lunch.

Upon arriving at the Amtra Travel office, we interrupted the overly busy office staff and were offered a cup of tea by Ms. Saovaluk. She had made reservations for our three-night stay at the Mansion Kempinski; arranged transportation to and from the airport; booked our flights from Bangkok to Hanoi, from Hanoi to Ho Chi Minh City, and from Ho Chi Minh City back to Bangkok; plus reserved another night's lodging at the Bangkok Airport Hotel. (We would have loved to have returned to the Kempinski, but with such an early morning departure flight from Bangkok to Taipei, it wasn't practical.) We paid $1289 in US traveler's checks for the lodging, airport transportation, and the airline tickets. Using a credit card would have incurred a sur-charge. Of course, we couldn't make airline reservations to, from, and within Vietnam before leaving the United States, so we were grateful for their services. Ms. Saovaluk recommended that her office secure the Vietnamese visas for us. I said that we would get our own visas. We wanted the experience. We were curious about how the Vietnamese Embassy looked, and we wanted to see it. I thought, no problem. After all, we had already applied for the visas, sent passport pictures, and had in our possession an official letter from UNDP with our visa request numbers. This would be a snap. After all, I was traveling for UNDP and the Ministry of Education in Vietnam. Wrong! How naive we were.

Amtra's driver transported us to this small dull bluish-gray building almost directly across the street from the plush United States Embassy compound. The main door to the embassy's public transaction office appeared to be falling off its hinges. There was no fancy lobby nor plush chairs with an attractive Vietnamese lady in her ao dai asking, "May I please help you?"

Instead we saw a bare cement floor, a ceiling fan laboring over a too crowded room. The air was hot, humid, and pungent from the two very long intertwining lines of people. Most of them appeared to be Thai and had their hands full of passports from various countries. Later we discovered that they were agents, securing visas for their clients. We should have listened to Ms. Saovaluk.

Linda got in the correct line. I got into the wrong one and was abruptly told, "No, next line." Linda hadn't moved one inch while I had worked myself to the front of the wrong line. I think all those ahead of me had been in the wrong line also. That's why our line moved so rapidly. After two hours and just as I finally got to the front of the proper line and showed my official UNDP letter with the proper visa number to the visa official, he looked at it, not at all impressed. In fact, he seemed very bored and handed me two applications for visas. I told him I had completed these applications many months ago in the US, and the UNDP office in Hanoi had submitted them to his office already. He remarked, "Must fill out application, now. Closed for lunch. Open at 13:30." I started to make a statement, pleading my case, but the sliding window was closed on me. I temporarily had a notion to turn into the Ugly American. Instead, I turned to Linda and said, "Here is another application. Better fill it out. I'll fill out mine, and we'll stay here and hold our place in line for the next hour and a half." Most of the people in line had left to get lunch. Only a handful stayed.

Just as I thought I had the situation in hand, the man directly behind me in line, said, "You must attach photos to visa applications and have extra photos available." I remarked that this was my second

16

visa application and that I had already mailed plenty of photos from Phoenix, Arizona.

Our helpful, new friend replied, "Better play the game and get new passport photos." Where would we get passport photos in the next hour, without losing our places in line? Our counselor remarked, "I just got mine at the corner of the main intersection, in a tiny hut marked, 'Passport Photos for Vietnam'." Sounded like a fishy business to me. I asked Linda to hold our places, while I returned to the streets of sweltering Bangkok. I cautiously avoided several vendors who accosted me as I walked down several blocks to a main thoroughfare, where I did indeed spot a street sign advertising Vietnam Visa Photos. I reluctantly looked into the open shop and inquired about photo opportunities. I was assured they could quickly take my picture, which they did for a small fee. I hurried back to the embassy, photos in hand, to give Linda specific directions to the photo shop. As I watched my wife disappear on her visa photo adventure, I was extremely apprehensive, and only felt at ease when she reappeared with her photos.

For the next hour Linda and I made the acquaintance and talked with a young master sergeant in the US Air Force, who was part of the American M.I.A. office in Hanoi, nicknamed, "The Ranch." I asked him if the Vietnamese Government was as competent and friendly as this visa office, concerning our hunt for American MIA's. To my surprise, he said the government of Vietnam was cooperating one hundred percent, and he had no

17

complaints whatsoever.  I told him my mission and said I definitely wanted to see the infamous "Hanoi Hilton." He said that could easily be done, as the prison is in downtown Hanoi.  We reminisced about Senator John McCain's imprisonment.  I related how I had met Col. George Day, who was also a POW and formerly lived in  Glendale, Arizona.   The master sergeant was a fine young man, extremely friendly and helpful.  He said he really enjoyed his job, which he had secured because of his fluency in Vietnamese, but he missed his wife and family, who remained in Hawaii for the six months he was based in Hanoi.        Much to our surprise, the window did open promptly at 13:30.  I was first in line and excitedly presented the newly filled-out visa applications plus the required photos, only to be told I must pay a fee of one thousand baht, (Thai money, equal to $40.00 US). I only had 700 baht in my wallet.  The young master sergeant stepped forward and gallantly offered to give me 300 baht.  The Vietnamese embassy official became very impatient and instructed me to bring 300 more baht the next morning at 8:30 A.M., and we would actually receive the long-awaited visas.  By now we had begun to figure out the system.  Upon our return to the Kempinski, I hurriedly changed a traveler's check for baht and then gave the Amtra driver the required 300 baht plus our passports and relievedly asked that he secure our visas the following morning.   We were hesitant to surrender our passports and try to function in Bangkok without them. Linda and I had wasted two-thirds of a day anticipating a new and meaningful experience.   It was a lesson learned.   Nervously, we sweated out the rest of the day, sightseeing. Linda insisted we have afternoon tea at the famous Oriental Hotel, so we listened to a flute and guitar concert, while we enjoyed high tea in the Oriental's Palm Court. Linda was reminded that the last time she had formal high tea was with our daughter Carin at the Phoenician in Scottsdale. We tried to make reservations for a Thai dinner, followed by a performance of Thai dancers, but it was sold out as it was Valentine's Day. We then took a two-hour taxi ride across town back to the lovely Mansion Kempinski. It was rush hour and we experienced the most horrendous traffic we'd ever encountered. The bumper to bumper lines of small sedans, tuk tuks, taxis, and motorbikes inched along in every direction. It was virtual gridlock, and the majority of motorcycle riders as well as pedestrians, were wearing face masks to protect themselves from breathing the extreme pollution.

At the hotel we learned of another place, the Bon Thai, which served dinner with Thai folk dancers. The show was extremely interesting with beautifully costumed lovely women. Unfortunately, the food didn't match the performance. We found our shoes, left previously at the door of the restaurant, put them on, flagged down a taxi, and returned to the hotel for our last night's stay at the Kempinski.

The next morning it was an absolute relief to finally regain our passports and obtain our much sought after visas, knowing we were fully approved to travel to Vietnam. We had prevailed. We won the battle of the visas.

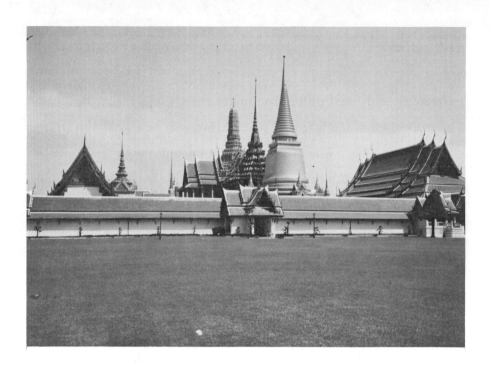

Wat Po Temple, Bangkok, Thailand

Grand Palace grounds, Bangkok, Thailand

# Chapter Two

## TOUCHDOWN HANOI

It was rather strange, I thought, to board a Vietnamese aircraft that had no markings at all, parked on the tarmac at the Bangkok International Airport. We had gone through the very efficient process of having our luggage bound by the Thai security people and had completed the customs and immigration procedures. We then enjoyed walking through the terminal and browsed the many interesting shops. Linda was particularly taken with the Thai handicrafts. We saw the entire terminal, because the gate for Vietnam Airlines was in the last section of the airport. We noticed a quiet and serious mood of the people in the waiting area at the gate, unlike most airports where there is much talking, laughing, and sometimes even boisterous activity.

We boarded a completely stark white aircraft. Welcoming us aboard, were several beautiful young Vietnamese ladies dressed in their colorful and charming ao dais; long white pants covered with a fitted coat/dress of a contrasting solid color and slit up the side to the waist. The attendants made us feel comfortable and during the flight they served us a box lunch of undeterminable food, except for the rice and a warm soft drink. I passed on the lunch and tried the warm soda but didn't like or even recognize the flavor, so that too was left to be picked up.

I positioned my head against the aircraft window as the French pilot explained our flight. My imagination began working immediately, and I wondered if we were flying over or near the Ia Drang Valley, where the men of the U.S. famed 7th Cavalry fought and died in the bloody Pleiku campaign. It has been written that this was the battle that changed the war in Vietnam. I actually said a prayer for all the men: U.S. and Vietnamese, who lost their lives and bloodied the soil in that valley. I now pray for those veterans, from both sides, who must live with the memory of this carnage that they witnessed and in which they participated. God bless them.

Vietnam looked beautiful from the air. It appeared so peaceful and calm. I wondered how life was going to be in Vietnam. Dozens of questions were racing through my inquisitive and apprehensive mind. How were the Vietnamese people going to react to these two Americans? Would I see any reminders of the war? Would I want to see anything concerning the war? Would my Vietnamese educator colleagues mention the war?

Suddenly, we received notice from a lovely crew member that we were minutes away from landing at the Hanoi airport. We would be leaving Seats 17H and K in economy class on Vietnam Airlines. I ceremoniously pinched myself, then Linda, and said, "You are in

Vietnam, Babe." As Linda gave me her "settle down, Chuck" look, I excitedly told her to lean over and take a look at some Vietnamese MIG fighter aircraft parked on the tarmac, which I could see as our plane streaked down from the clouds through the misty, cloudy sky. They looked very unfamiliar and unfriendly, as I viewed the bright red star painted on the silver tail. This time, Linda gave me her disgusted look. I had already been informed by her that we were not coming to Vietnam to study, seek information on, nor investigate anything connected with the war that took place twenty years ago. She did not turn her head to look at the Russian-built Mig fighter aircraft nor feel the least bit cheated about having missed this military sight. Linda had repeatedly told me she wanted to see Vietnam in the present, experience its culture, and meet the Vietnamese people. She certainly didn't want to be reminded of the war. By now, we had landed and the engines of the aircraft were stopped. We deplaned by the old-fashioned roller stairs and boarded a shuttle bus that transported us to the terminal.

As we left the shuttle and entered the terminal, I felt I had stepped back in time about thirty-five years. The building was small, bare, dark, and damp. We were then told to fill out our customs and immigration forms and line up at counters to present our passports, before we could even think of our luggage. I joked with Linda that if it was not done right, perhaps we would spend our stay at the Hanoi Hilton. This time I received the "You are not one bit funny"

23

look. We then both spotted a lovely, familiar, and very welcome face. It was Delores Morey with a luggage cart and her driver, motioning us to get in a different line and proceed to the baggage retrieval area. After hugs and being presented a bouquet of gladiolus, we got the luggage and were seated in Delores' car. Then her driver scared the daylights out of me, as he dodged, swerved, and drove through a mass of bicycles and small motorcycles on the new highway leading from the airport to downtown Hanoi. I just knew he was going to hit someone or cause an accident. With horn blaring, we sped down the new highway past fields of rice paddies, guarded by water buffaloes.

During the hour-long drive we saw miles and miles of rice paddies, water buffaloes, and the Vietnamese villagers in their conical straw hats. We crossed the famous Red River. Now we felt we really were in Vietnam. It was cool, misty, cloudy, and a dreary rain was falling. The weather was gloomy but did not dampen our spirits. I thought I saw what I perceived to be shanty after shanty. It seemed like tremendous poverty was gripping this area. I did see hundreds and hundreds of entrepreneurs. Everything imaginable was being sold on the side of the roads in the country and in the streets of downtown Hanoi. Delores pointed out the UN compound, where many of the UN employees lived. It looked very modern. We also saw the Swiss, Russian, and Cuban Embassies. I noted that there were dozens of identical businesses, one right after the other, down both sides of the street. On another street, a different series of identical businesses

24

would be lined up, side by side. Delores explained that this is the way it is in Hanoi. One particular block would be occupied by motorcycle repair shops. The next street might have shops that sold only shirts; that was shirt street. We saw hat street, silver street, TV street, lamp street, furniture street, and on and on. It was both interesting and practical. You better know the street that sells the item you wish to purchase; otherwise, it might be quite confusing.

We finally arrived at Roy and Delores' home, the residence of the UNDP Resident Representative. From the outside it looked all that had been described by Carolyn, Roy and Delores' daughter and my Godchild. She and her husband Teall related this to us after they had returned home to New York City from a visit with her parents the previous summer. They both said, "You won't believe it." They were right. I could not believe it. Sitting on a corner of a very picturesque area of Hanoi, and just across the street from a university, was the residence that once had been occupied by the Soviet High Military Command during the war. The Soviets left, and the villa remained vacant for some time. It was one of few sites available, although needing renovation when the Moreys were assigned to Vietnam from Beijing, China. Roy and Delores had informed Linda and me that this magnificent structure needed extensive renovation before they could move into it. They designed and supervised the remodeling of this very large two story villa - a process which took four months to complete. Today, it is probably the finest diplomatic residence in all Hanoi, bar none.

After driving through the outside gate and entering the back entrance of the residence, Delores instructed us to follow their custom to remove our shoes and put on felt slippers to walk into the home. What a delightful custom. It not only helps keep the marble floors clean, but also reduces wear and tear on the large, beautiful Chinese and Vietnamese carpets. Touring the home, we observed the ultra-large living room, dining room, kitchen, and Chinese-style bedroom plus two bathrooms downstairs. We climbed the staircase of many steps, as each of the two floors have eighteen-foot high ceilings, and were shown our room with its own private bath. As we circled the upstairs, we viewed the master bedroom plus bath and dressing room, office, TV/family room, second guest room, large storage area, laundry room, and two more bathrooms. I remarked to Delores, "You've come a long way, Baby!", as we all recalled Cottage City, the married housing complex consisting of two-room structures of malapai rock and renting for $35 a month, where we had all lived as married college students in 1958. I didn't have the courage to ask about the monthly rent to the Vietnamese Government for this great villa. Anyway, I was prepared to enjoy it for the next week. I also fully intended to use all seven bathrooms at one time or another. This was a special luxury, as we reminded each other of the lack of toilet facilities on the annual camping expeditions through northern New Mexico, southern Colorado, and the Navajo and Hopi Reservations.

Roy was driven home in his staff car by his driver, and I quickly began to tease and remind him about his driving days, when he was a young student working summers driving a truck for an Arizona copper mining company. It is a good thing all of us have been close friends for over 34 years. We can tease and joke with each other about anything. Roy offered me a choice of a San Miguel beer or a Canada Dry tonic water before dinner. I decided on the tonic water, since he didn't have a Corona. We would have our Coronas next summer. For now, it was a tonic water imported from Hong Kong. Roy humorously invited us into the dining room to sit and dine our first night in Hanoi with the UNDP Resident Representative and his wife. I told Roy I would just as soon have a bologna sandwich to go with the tonic water, in the living room. Roy laughed as Linda gave me the Chuuuuck look. The four of us sat at one end of the elegant fourteen-place dining room table, surrounded by part of the Morey's fine collection of American and Oriental art. The Vietnamese cook prepared and then graciously served us a lovely French dinner, including cheese souffle. It was a first-rate evening meal with conversation that set the tone for the rest of our stay in Hanoi.

After much fabulous discussion, reminiscing, and after-dinner coffee, it was off to bed. Linda and I unpacked and lay in bed listening to the sounds of Hanoi, trying to convince ourselves that we were with Roy and Delores in Hanoi, Vietnam. This makes the third exotic and exciting site we have shared with them outside the United States. The first was in Geneva, Switzerland, when Roy was U.S. Deputy Assistant Secretary of State. The second was Beijing, China. I knew that the coming days would hold a wonderful adventure. It was exciting just reading the itinerary Roy had given me, but I was going to actually experience it firsthand. Linda dropped off to sleep, but I law awake thinking, "What is this guy from Durango, Colorado, and Winslow, Arizona, doing here?" This was a far cry and an ocean away from "standin' on a corner in Winslow, Arizona."

After a wonderfully casual breakfast, Delores took Linda and me to UNDP headquarters to visit Roy in his office and meet his staff. It was gratifying to make the acquaintance of people whom we had corresponded with by fax transmissions and phone conversations. I followed Roy to his UNDP conference room and took photos at the head of the conference table, of course. Roy took me to his office and gave me a briefing on the geography of Vietnam from his wall map. He began to show me where I would travel and what I would see. It was very stimulating, and I was excited to begin. I was ready to orient myself, with the help of a driver and interpreter to the intriguing city of Hanoi. I was now going to travel the city that had been in the back of every American's mind for the past twenty years. Many Americans wanted it obliterated; others would love to see it, feel it, smell it, and travel this historical city that had held our wartime fliers for almost a decade.

Linda excused herself out of my "war exorcism journey" to something more genteel. She was accompanying Delores to the Indonesian Embassy for a farewell luncheon, hosted by the wife of the Ambassador of Indonesia. They were leaving their assignment in Vietnam for the same post in Beijing, China.

The first request I made of the driver was to take me to the Hao Lo Prison, built by the French in 1898. (Commonly referred to as "Hanoi Hilton" by Americans during the war, it was completely razed by November of 1994.) I wanted desperately to walk the inside to see the cells and visualize the days and times of George Day, Senator McCain, Alvarez, and all the other captured American fliers I had read about and prayed for all those years. The visit was not to be. The Vietnamese government is not particularly interested in anyone visiting this site that still exists as a prison for its own citizens now. As we circled the city block which contained the stronghold inside downtown Hanoi, my piercing eyes took in each flake of dark, musty, yellow paint chip of the ten to twelve feet thick walls with guard towers in the corners. The driver parked near the entrance, and I got out and motioned sheepishly to a guard, if I could enter. He looked at me strangely and gave me his sign language for an abrupt NO! I asked if I could take photographs of the entrance. The guard looked at me like I was nuts and was probably thinking, "Only you weird, dumb Americans would ever want a picture of this miserable place." I also found it interesting to take pictures of some Russian made Army vehicles parked in front of the prison. Again, the guards looked at me strangely, made some statements in Vietnamese, and laughed. They were making some pretty comical statements about me, judging from their laughter.

The driver asked me where I would like to go next. Did I have another spot to visit? Somewhere I had once read that there was a sculpture dedicated to the capture of Senator John McCain. I mentioned John McCain to the driver, and he readily nodded his head and repeated over and over, "Ma-Keen, Ma-Keen, ah yes, Ma-Keen, Ma-Keen." He speeded up the Toyota and soon we arrived at a beautiful lake with excursion boats, picnic areas, beautiful walkways, and a pavilion with food and drink stands plus a lounge area. The driver made a parking spot for the car and directed me to the sculpture, just off a sidewalk on the bank of the lake. I recognized an abstract flat sculpture of a man bound in chains, hanging with bent knees. On the left side of the sculpture is a broken wing of an aircraft with the letters, USAF. Passersby, young and old, stopped to watch me take pictures of this statue from several different angles. The driver must have thought I was funny, as he laughed. The small group stopped laughing, particularly the few who understood English, when they heard my announcement to the driver. I told him there was a very serious error in that sculpture. He surprisingly and half-frightened and embarrassedly asked what the error was. I walked to

30

the sculpture and fingered the letters USAF and announced that John McCain was a US Navy pilot. It should be USN, not USAF. That group of people looked at each other puzzledly; then looked at me as if I had just closed down their amusement area. There was an error, and I had pointed it out. What else is an old teacher to do in such a situation? I evaluated the project, graded the results, and pointed out the mistake. Someone got a C+ for the project, and that is just the expression I visualized with this diverse crowd of Vietnamese. They all thought they had earned an A. I awarded a C+.

By this hour of the morning it was time to keep my luncheon appointment so the driver whisked me from the McCain sculpture to UNDP headquarters. I just knew we would literally kill at least one dozen of his countrymen on bicycles, motorcycles, or cyclos, (the Vietnamese-style rickshaws), before we reached our destination. As I gripped the armrest with one hand and dug my finger nails into the seat, I said some prayers and asked for forgiveness and mercy on those drivers of bicycles, motorcycles, and cyclos, who were about to lose their lives. I couldn't believe that we reached UNDP headquarters and were waved into the compound without one fatality, mishap, or collision. We did; however, experience several hundred near misses, and I had several hundred more gray hairs on my head.

I raced up the stairs to let Roy know I was there for lunch. He gave some instructions to his staff, and we boarded his personal UNDP staff car. This time we both sat in the back seat, and I sat

31

directly behind the driver, as Roy sat in his official spot in the car, according to practice, that is; back seat directly behind the rider's front seat, right-rear. I looked at Roy and stated, "Come on, Roy, just for me."

Roy said, "I knew you would ask." So, out came the UN car flag, flying from the right front fender, as we were driven off to my first lunch in a Hanoi establishment. I looked at the building we were about to enter and thought, "Roy isn't trying to impress me much with this restaurant." The building looked like it could use a paint job, as did the majority of the buildings in Hanoi, which is not surprising, given the year round high humidity. It also could have used a cleaning, new floors, reconstructed staircase, and new furniture. The first two floors of the building housed an art exhibit of local artists. It was very different art, but I liked it. Much of it was water color landscapes. I thought it both colorful and representative of the country.

As we reached our table, the thought grabbed me again, "Chuck, you're about to have a Vietnamese lunch, smack dab in the middle of Hanoi, the capital and nerve center of the Vietnam government, and within walking distance of the 'Hanoi Hilton." I reminded myself that it has been decades since conflict existed between the United States and Vietnamese forces. Why do I keep floating back? There is no real reason for it, except curiosity and history. I tend to be fascinated by Vietnam. It was such an intense, controversial, and vivid part of recent American history.

The first thing I sampled in this Vietnamese restaurant was a cashew nut, a local product that is very popular and grows naturally in Vietnam. No doubt about it, these were the finest cashews I had ever tasted. Roy was absolutely correct when the previous summer while camping in Colorado, he had stated, "You haven't eaten nuts until you taste the Vietnamese cashews," as we sipped Coronas and ate almonds during our happy hour, overlooking the Swiss-style village of Ouray. We had just begun to formulate plans for our trip to Vietnam.

Roy asked, "What'll you have, my friend?"

I said, "You order, Roy," since I was not able to make much sense out of the Vietnamese menu. Roy ordered the following for each of us: onion soup, a pork dish, a bowl of noodles, (of course,) French fries, (The strong French influence remains, even after all this time.), tonic water, and banana flambe' for dessert. I may have been critical of the building and lack of ambience, but I could never be negative about the meal. The food was delicious and the company was a special friend of thirty-nine years. We had shared many and diverse experiences. What more could two long-time buddies ask for? After Roy paid the bill in Vietnamese dong instead of the coveted US dollars, he decided we would spend the rest of this two-hour lunch period, (what a great custom!), showing me some quick sites nearby. We walked to the exclusive, newly remodeled Metropole Hotel. It is

33

now as modern and trendy as any luxurious hotel should be. It would be nice to spend a night here, but I was told that one must book reservations months and months, maybe even a year, in advance. Roy said, even he was often unable to reserve rooms for official foreign diplomats. It had always been full. He then walked me to the site where Ho Chi Minh gave his famous speech in 1945, when he quoted Abraham Lincoln's Gettysburg Address, the American Declaration of Independence, and the U.S. Constitution. I love the historical aspects of this nation and, of course, had my picture taken there.

After our two-hour lunch was gone, and we had returned to Roy's office, he instructed his driver to take me to his residence and then return to his office. There was no UN flag flying this time, because Roy was not in the car. Oh well!

At the residence I transferred into Delores' car. Linda came with me this time to tour the Ho Chi Minh Museum. This is a massive Soviet style structure. The largest Vietnamese flag I have ever seen was flying from a forty to fifty foot tall flag pole at the entrance of the museum. Immediately inside, the first item one sees upon entering is a large likeness of Ho Chi Minh, himself. This revered leader is very much respected by the Vietnamese people. There were no public buildings and very few private buildings that did not have a large picture of "Uncle Ho" displayed.

On every floor was a substantial amount of Vietnamese abstract art. It had historical significance as the art is representative of the government, political ideology, and culture of the country. There were, of course, typical displays depicting victories of the Vietnamese army over the Chinese, the French, and finally, the Americans. I viewed captured American flight suits, helicopter helmets, US M-16 rifles, US GI helmets, US GI boots, US bayonets and trench knives, and various pieces of US aircraft. It was a very different sensation for patriotic American, me, to see these captured items on display in a museum. I understood, but it was somewhat disturbing, realizing these few items symbolized the tremendous toll of human casualties produced by the war, on all sides; American as well as both North and South Vietnamese. I guess that's why Linda didn't spend much time taking in these displays. She found these displays to be sad and morbid. I found her outside, surveying the beautifully landscaped and lush grounds. Across a large lawn was a walkway leading to the Ho Chi Minh Mausoleum. Ho Chi Minh is more than a dead leader, hero, or official. He is almost god-like in the homage he is paid. His spirit is still very much alive among the citizens, who solemnly visit the mausoleum. We were turned away, for it was closed that day.

On our return to the UNDP residence, we were driven past many Vietnamese government administrative buildings, foreign embassies, and private business establishments, by the dozens. We saw lots of construction. Also we passed "shirt street," "silk street," "silver street," "motorbike street," "electronic equipment street," "bicycle street," and "fresh produce street." On almost any corner we could see small carts, now empty, that earlier in the day had sold small loaves of French bread for the equivalent of about five American cents. There were shops of all description, but of course no shopping malls. That possibility for American joint venture had not yet begun, as the trade embargo had so recently been lifted. Somehow or another, I cannot get excited about seeing a Target, Walgreen's, Circle K, and Safeway grouped into a shopping center near Lenin Park, the Metropole, Sword Lake, or UNDP Headquarters. It would certainly usurp the Vietnamese ambience.

Upon returning to the Morey home, Delores informed me that a lady who regularly gives massages, would be arriving soon, and would I be interested in having a full body massage. I must have appeared rather unworldly and unsophisticated when I admitted to Delores that I had never received a massage. I asked somewhat bewilderedly what it entailed. Delores explained that it would be given on the bed I was using, and I should undress down to my jockeys and let the 45 minute experience begin. Linda passed, as she doesn't even care to have her back rubbed, but I quickly undressed to my underwear and lay face down on the covered bed, already prepared by the housekeeper to prevent oil from soiling the bed spread. The Vietnamese lady, a friend of the housekeeper and masseuse to Delores, walked into the bedroom. She was wearing immaculate white pants, a pink blouse, and long white coat. She looked like a physician or a nurse. She appeared to be in her mid thirties to early forties, though I am terrible at age estimation, American or Vietnamese. She was pleasant, though non verbal with me, of course. She did not speak one word of English. She had strong hands and was very skilled, gentle but firm, and the massage was extremely professional and thorough. As this was my very first massage, (Linda hates to even rub my back), I was thoroughly intrigued by the technique and art of the complete massage she executed. She kneaded, pounded, rubbed, or pummeled the entire surface of my body, even massaging my scalp. She indicated that I should turn over so she could repeat these same motions on the front of my body. She only skipped two items, my buttocks and groin area. I'd wondered about these areas until it was over. As I finally sat up, covered with a pleasant layer of oil, thoroughly relaxed and totally uninhibited, she somewhat shyly stated, "three dollow." I could not believe the very low fee, as I walked to the dresser to get three US one dollar bills from my wallet. I later understood that I had saved about $47 by experiencing this very satisfying event in Vietnam, rather than in the United States. American "experts" could certainly learn from this Vietnamese lady, and I was quickly thinking how I could convince her to come to Phoenix, Arizona, USA.

After a quick shower, Delores informed us that dinner was about to be served. During the meal, Roy asked if I had enjoyed the massage.

"Absolutely," I answered, as Roy related that after a hard day at the office, he missed his massage because of a guest at the residence. I told Roy I hoped he would miss many more of his massages in the next few days while his guest remained at his residence. We both remarked how it would have been luxurious to experience this massage back in 1955, when we both ended bruised and battered from two-a-day football drills on old Lumberjack Field at Arizona State College in Flagstaff, Arizona. How we would have loved to have been so pampered before dropping into our bunks in Bury Hall, dreading having to endure the same punishment the following day, and the next, and the next. There was even more "remember when" conversation, as we four sat in the dining room, with dinner being served and savoring every delicious bite, as we intermittently sipped a dry French wine, chosen by Roy especially for this occasion. Roy and Delores believed me when I said I would come to Hanoi if I could be wined and dined. We laughed, teased, and remembered, as the four of us sat and thought back almost four decades, with six children and nine grandchildren between us, plus so many shared experiences. Roy looked at me, winked, and repeated the statement he had first made to us, as we had enjoyed lunch in a penthouse overlooking the Alps in Geneva, Switzerland, almost 20 years before. "Not bad for a kid from Marana, huh?"

I smiled and made my usual response to him. "You bet, and not bad for a kid from Winslow, either." (Roy and Delores had graduated from Marana High School in a tiny farming community, just north of Tucson, while I had received my diploma from Winslow High School, in a little larger desert town on the edge of the Navajo Indian Reservation in northern Arizona. Linda is not of our small town variety. She had gone to the sophisticated North Phoenix High School in the capital of Arizona.)

Following dinner, Roy gave me a copy of a speech on education in Vietnam, which he had previously delivered. It was homework time. He also gave me the results of a UNDP Educational Survey that his office had researched for the country of Vietnam. He then asked me for a copy of the major address I was to deliver the next day at the Ministry of Education for the Government of Vietnam. He informed me a car and driver would be available for all my official visits to the Ministry of Education, the universities, and colleges. The Government of Vietnam would assign an interpreter for my every need.

As Linda and I prepared for bed in our private room on the second floor of what we began jokingly to refer to as the "Mansion Morey," we were both excited and filled with anticipation for what the next days and weeks would hold for us. It seemed so natural for me to be on this mission to Vietnam. I felt comfortable and believed this is what I was destined to do. As we settled into sleep, we heard loud Vietnamese being spoken out on the sidewalks surrounding the residence; we heard the large trucks rumbling through the streets at various times of the night; and we heard the constant ringing of the bicycle and cyclo bells, plus the loud unmuffled noise of the motorbikes, as they traveled the city. Interspersed through all these noises was the intermittent explosion of fire crackers. Tet, the Vietnamese New Year's celebration, was still being recognized, even though the official holiday was over. We managed to sleep in spite of all these distractions.

Chuck on steps of Ho Chi Minh Museum - Hanoi, Vietnam

John McCain, POW Statue - Hanoi, Vietnam

Hao Lo Prison - "Hanoi Hilton"

Streets of Hanoi

Ho Chi Minh Museum - Hanoi Vietnam

# Chapter Three

# THE MINISTRY

After an informal and quiet but friendly breakfast, I studied my official itinerary for working day one. I was to meet and address the Ministry of Education at 10:00 A.M. and make a major presentation at 14:00 hours. The first man I was scheduled to meet was the First Vice-Minister of Education, Mr. Pham Minh Hac. The interpreter accompanying me would be Miss Phung Hoang Anh of the official Foreign Economic Relations Department, Office of the Government of Vietnam. Le Huu Cat Dien, the National Programme Officer of the United Nations Development Programme, completed the entourage.

Linda bade me farewell, Delores winked, and the housekeeper, Lap, shyly smiled as I was driven off. I sat in Roy's spot in the back seat of the vehicle with Cat Dien, and Miss Anh was in front with the driver. I felt like an American envoy off on a mission in Vietnam as I was driven through the guard gate into the compound of the Ministry of Education. Inside, the driver was too quick for me, as he jumped out of the car and opened the door. This little competition to open the door first, was carried out during my entire stay in Hanoi. I vowed I would be victorious in the contest to

43

open the door, once the vehicle was at a complete stop. I never won the race of the door opening.

There were several dignitaries on the top steps of the Ministry of Education building, waiting to greet me as I stepped from the vehicle. Formal introductions were made by Miss Anh. I stepped forward as each official was introduced to me and shook hands, warmly smiled, and did a quarter of a body and head bow. I was following their every move. After this initial courtesy, I was gently led into the building and immediately faced a large portrait of "Uncle Ho." We walked down a cold, semi-lit hallway to a reception room, where, anticipating my arrival, there had been placed a tray of China with several hot pots of tea, cookies, oranges, tangerines, and bananas. I was then formally introduced to my host, Dr. Bui Cong Tho, Vice Director of the International Cooperation Department of the Ministry of Education and Training. The second gentleman to whom I was presented was Ta The-Truyen, English Ph.D. and Director of Continuing Education, Department of the Ministry of Education and Training. After a short conversation of greeting which included compliments, appreciative comments, and toasts of tea, I presented a large pewter plate, engraved with Northern Arizona University, 1899, encircling a facsimile of "Old Main," to the Ministers of Education, the Ministry of Education and Training, and to all educators of Vietnam from the president, faculty, staff, and students of Northern Arizona University in Flagstaff, Arizona, USA.

All was very impressive, I thought, but I soon learned that the

44

art of conversation and the delivery of an address were compounded into a very difficult state, because by using an interpreter, one can neither make a complete statement nor voice a complete thought. One must allow the interpreter to comprehend the message, retain the message, then translate that message after converting languages to a comprehensible thought. This whole process is very complicated. I love to talk, so Miss Anh had her work cut our for her. I really tried to make the situation as smooth as possible. I tried to keep track of my message and allow her to translate properly to my colleagues. There is even the difficulty of trying to translate an American word or phrase that does not have Vietnamese translation. The whole business of interpreting and translation is complicated and can be stressful. Miss Anh was excellent and did a fine job. The more we worked together, the better team we became. I hated to see Miss Anh, my interpreter, leave, when her assignment was completed.

I then presented miniature "Lumberjack" lapel pins to all the educators I met. Somewhere in a classroom or office is an instructor wearing a "Lumberjack" pin, depicting the mascot of Northern Arizona University. (I know they are being worn, because the next day I saw a man with the pin on his lapel where I had pinned it the previous day.)

In the afternoon after the traditional two-hour lunch at the Morey's with Linda, I addressed the ministers and staff of the Ministry of Education. They questioned me at length about continuing education practices in the United States, university curriculum, bachelor's degree and graduate degree requirements, grading practices, entrance requirements, fees and expenses, majors and minors, vocational education, etc. Their questions were well thought out, very intelligent, and generally in tune with the world of education. The Vietnamese hold scholars in high esteem, and in earlier times, competition in education was how Vietnamese citizens of all social classes rose to offices within the government. I almost entertained the thought that these wise men were checking out our American system just to determine how far we had progressed. With the affirmative nodding of heads and smiles every so often, I surmised they approved of my answers and information, and that they were pleased and excited by what I proposed.

I was questioned at great length by the leader of this assembly, Dr. Nguyen Nhat Quang, the deputy director of the Continuing Education Department of the Ministry of Education and Training. During my talk, I was served the traditional Vietnamese hot tea in very small, demitasse-like cups. I tried desperately to act the good guest and sipped between statements of interpretation. I no more than finished the tea, when I was served the "popular drink of Vietnam," Coca Cola. Just as we arrived in Vietnam, soon after President Clinton had lifted the trade embargo, Coca Cola initiated a marketing campaign in Vietnam that was comical, outrageous, and effective. All the remainder of our stay in Hanoi, I saw Coca Cola on every table. A large red and white vinyl Coca Cola banner was

46

hung across the stately Opera House. There was also a similar one hung from the trees surrounding the Morey's residence. We thought these placements a bit tacky. I didn't check to see if Coca Cola had snuck up on the Ho Chi Minh Mausoleum. Even the smallest, most modest noodle shop had a sign hanging in their living quarters. I thought of whether I would like this in my living room. Coca Cola was on the lips of every Vietnamese and became the drink to drink. I popped the can, leaned back, and thought, this is unreal. I am addressing the Education Ministry, my interpreter is working very diligently, and I have a cool Coke in my hand, refreshing myself, . . . in Hanoi. I have to give the marketing people of Coca Cola credit. I thought their slogan was great! The Coca Cola script on one end of the elongated banner was traditional. On the other end were the Vietnamese words, translated for me as, "Glad to see you again." I loved it. I hoped Pepsi wouldn't take offense. I had heard that on the day the embargo was lifted, the Pepsi Co. gave away free drinks of Pepsi that had been bottled in Ho Chi Minh City. That was quite a coup. The Coca Cola I had seen and been offered everywhere was imported from Singapore or Bangkok.

I was reluctant to leave the directors, but the end of the work day was coming to a close. We had not had one power outage, and I was finished with my tea and Coke. The officers applauded me enough to inflate my ego, and several shook my hand, making me feel I was effective. I was both stimulated and satisfied. I realized then that the government of Vietnam clearly wants to emphasize education and standardize it for the masses.

After Cat Dien and Miss Anh delivered me back to the UNDP residence, I excitedly related my experiences to Roy, Delores, and Linda. I suggested to Linda that she should accompany me on some of my itinerary to get the real flavor of what my mission to Vietnam was about, and how I was being received. I thought she would find it fascinating to meet some of these interesting people, have some tea, and try a Coke.

The dinner this evening proved to be just as thrilling as the day of meetings had been. Roy and Delores had sent formal invitations to a dinner they were hosting in our honor. We initially learned of this special occasion our first evening in Hanoi, when we noticed our copy of the invitation on the dresser in our room.

The Resident Representative of

The United Nations Development Programme

In the Social Republic of Viet Nam

and Mrs. Roy D. Morey

request the pleasure of your company to

Dinner, on Thursday, 17 February 1994 at 7:00 P.M.

2 Ly Thuong Kiet, Hanoi

RSVP

There were ten guests from the UNDP community who welcomed Linda and me and made us feel genuinely happy that we were in

Hanoi. Roy's toast was initially formal, but he also managed to be personal and witty. It was great fun to be entertained in this lovely old French villa, where all fourteen places were filled at the banquet table. We felt very special. We were grateful to see Jia, a Chinese lady whom we had first met in Beijing, when she had accompanied us to the Peking Opera. Now, she was working for UNDP in Hanoi, on a temporary leave from Beijing. We had already met Cat Dien when he accompanied me to my first round of meetings this morning. Liuga had originally been with Roy in Samoa and was helpful to the Moreys in being able to attain this wonderful villa and have it renovated. It was particularly fascinating to visit with him and learn that he is a Samoan chief, the leader of his clan. Jordan had also been in China, but came after our visit there. Nevertheless, we had heard about his marriage to Ching the previous spring, when Delores attended their wedding in Beijing. Even now, we weren't able to meet Ching, as she was visiting her physician in Hong Kong, receiving pre-natal care for the birth of their baby. Delores even gave us all permission to wear leather shoes on her marble floors and exquisite Chinese carpets. After a nightcap with just the four of us, Delores proposed, and I insisted that Linda go with me the next morning on my visitation.

As I lay in our bedroom that night, feeling so very far away from home, my memory bank brought up my very first "far from home" trip. It was a Boy Scout camping trip on the banks of Oak Creek, on what is now the site of touristy Tlaquepaque in Sedona,

Arizona. That night I stared at the stars and marvelled that I was over sixty miles away from home, deep in a canyon, in the middle of the forest. Only a few miles away, the movie BROKEN ARROW starring Jimmy Stewart was being filmed. I had sneaked onto the set where some night scenes were being filmed. I felt I was a man of the world then, away from home, sleeping under the stars, and having just witnessed Hollywood in action. Now, many years later, I was in Hanoi, Vietnam, being feted by international and government officials. What else was there?

Today, Friday, I am scheduled to meet with Professor Dr. Hoang Duc Nhuan, the Director General of the National Institute for Education Science of Vietnam and Director of Population, Environmental Aids and Drug Education Programme at the Teachers Training College of Hanoi and the Education Sciences Institute. Linda and I walked into the conference room with the traditional, large photograph of Ho Chi Minh prominently displayed. We experienced our first of a series of power outages. There was no break in the discussion when they occurred, as Dr. Duc Nhuan and Miss Anh promptly rose and opened the shutters and doors for light. It would have been refreshing, except that it was raining, and the wind was blowing. The traditional tea was very welcome on this cool and breezy morning. I couldn't help but notice the beautifully carved window frames and the sculpted panels over the doors. These rooms once had to have been exquisite and grand. The building was old French architecture, as are many of the buildings in Hanoi. They were mouldy and in need of a scrubbing and/or paint. Hanoi surely was at one time a splendid old French colonial city, with its Western European architecture, abundance of wrought iron, and wide boulevards. I would have loved to have seen it before the wars.

Dr. Duc Nhuan and I had a very informative discussion on the comparison of education in Vietnam and in the United States. He related to me that the general population of Vietnam is gaining in the bachelor degree programs, but is only maintaining in the master degree programs. There is a marked absence of young people with doctorate degrees, as most of the doctorate degrees are held by the older and retired generations. The war completely upset the educational system by destroying school buildings and dispatching teachers and scholars into wartime duties. Since the war, all schools, professional, technical, secondary, elementary, and special training schools, are sponsored and subsidized by the government. Dr. Nhuan also told me that recently some foreign organizations had begun helping the Vietnamese educational system by making sizable donations to expand and improve library facilities in schools throughout the country. Here was an outstanding Vietnamese educational leader who was well informed, modern and up-to-date on educational policies and practices. He would be a functional educator in any country. Upon my departure and after photographs and my awarding of the NAU gifts, he insisted that I take a generous supply of the Mandarin oranges that were served during our conference. I made my first street purchase in front of the Science Institute, when

51

I bought two large bouquets of gladiolus for one US dollar each, one for Linda and one to take to Delores. The Vietnamese ladies were both curious about us and grateful for our purchase. The only problem was, during the transaction, every flower peddler on the block came rushing toward us to also try to make a sale with these "wealthy Americans."

The driver, accompanied by our interpreter, drove us to the Ho Chi Minh Mausoleum. It was again closed. I don't know the reason for the closing that day. I figure the Vietnamese government heard Chuck Pilon was in town and wanted in, so they closed down. I hope to catch them off guard one future day. Bun then managed to take us to Van Mieu - Quoc Tu Giam, the center of cultural and scientific activities for Hanoi. It was also the first national University of Vietnam, founded in 1076 A.D. It thrived until 1779. The outstanding doctoral students' names are inscribed on large ancient tablets, almost like enlarged tombstones. Some of the tablets were mounted on giant turtles, carved from stone. This was a thriving advanced educational center during the American Revolutionary War. It was very impressive, even now, and a pious atmosphere permeated the garden walkways, ponds, and monuments, as the aroma of incense drifted out of the building which housed a series of Buddhas. Praying citizens were there paying homage. I felt highly flattered when Miss Anh placed incense sticks before one Buddha, bowed three times, and said, "For you and lady to have a happy and safe trip." This was a lovely gesture, and I was touched and honored. I tried to take pictures of two adorable little girls about four and five years old, who followed us all over the grounds. They continuously said, "Hallow," to us, and I always replied, "hello, hello." Yet, every time I attempted to focus the camera on them, they'd scamper off. I had to stop at the gift shop and buy two Han-Oi hand embroidered t-shirts for $8.00 US. Linda chastised me, as she had bought t-shirts at t-shirt block for half that. I've always been a poor shopper, but I still wanted these t-shirts and didn't want to go back to t-shirt block. It was cool and rainy, and the car was waiting to take us back to the Morey's for lunch. As we hurried to the car, four little feet pattered behind us and then stood on the street as we drove away. The little girls waved good-bye to us and yelled, "Hallow," one more time.

"Hello, hello precious little girls. Have a good life."

At the residence, I kicked off my shoes, put on my slippers, and ran upstairs to put the t-shirts in our room. Delores' housekeeper Lap had already washed, dried, and ironed my previous day's clothes. They were all neatly folded on the bed. What a lady! What a place!

Roy had arranged to take me to the Army Museum after lunch. This was one of the six national museums and established on 22 December, 1959, in the center of Hanoi near Lenin's statue as well as the Ho Chi Minh Mausoleum. The first thing I spotted on the grounds was the well-known ancient monument, Hanoi Flag Tower, a round, red-brick structure built on an elevated grassy plateau, overlooking the entire area. The construction of it, a national historic and cultural monument, took place from 1805 to 1812. The second display I noticed was a Vietnam Air Force MIG 21 and the wreckage of a US aircraft under the MIG. This exhibit made me feel strange and sad.

The Army Museum, using many exhibits, photographs, maps, and models, displays the history of the Vietnamese People's Armed Forces under the leadership of President Ho Chi Minh. One outstanding display was a scale model of Dien Bien Phu with a detailed description of how Vietnam defeated the French in 1954. Now, I finally understood how the Vietnamese supply routes were utilized along the Ho Chi Minh Trail, when I studied a pack-bicycle that was used in that effort. It appeared to be an ordinary bike, except that there was a long sturdy pole bound to one of the handle bars and another bound pole extended from the seat area of the bike. These adapted bicycles could then be loaded with hundreds and hundreds of pounds of supplies, as they were steered/walked down the Ho Chi Minh Trail. Another display that tugged at my heart was a large collection of artifacts from the air war over Hanoi from the 18th to the 29th of December, 1972, entitled "Dien Bien Phu in the Air." I saw pieces of wreckage with the United Stated Air Force insignias of the Strategic Air Command as well as the Tactical Air Command emblazoned on them. There were flight suits, helmets, survival gear, and weapons. I stood in front of the exhibit and said a prayer for someone, someplace, and their families, somewhere in the United States.

I then saw the Vietnamese tank that crashed through the Presidential Palace gate in Saigon on 30 April 1975, when the North declared the independence for all of Vietnam. Even the gate of the palace was placed symbolically under the tank that led this Ho Chi Minh campaign.

The display that really captured my attention was one dedicated to the capture of the first American serviceman, US Navy pilot Lt. Everett Alvarez from California. (My interest stemmed from the fact that he was born in Globe, a small town in Arizona.) I was given permission to pick up his flight suit, helmet, shoes, pieces of his aircraft, and picture of him in prison. As I did, it brought back vivid memories of many billboards I had seen in California immediately after his capture very early in the war, screaming, "FREE EVERETT ALVAREZ." I had said many a prayer for him, and they were eventually answered. Roy reminded me that when he was the UNDP Resident Representative in Western Samoa, he had met Alvarez, then the United States Peace Corps Director, and, in fact, he had hosted Alvarez for breakfast at his residence.

I grew quite nostalgic when I was allowed to pick up and read US pilot's names on dozens and dozens of flight helmets on display. I wondered about the whereabouts of these pilots and their dispositions now. Again, another prayer for the pilots and their families was offered.

There were very poignant picture displays of the Presidents Kennedy, Johnson, and Nixon, plus Secretary of State Kissinger, and

Secretary of Defense McNamara. The strain showed on all their faces as the war progressed. Many Vietnamese and Vietcong flags were on display. No "puppet" flags from the South were exhibited. This entire tour was quite emotional for me, and yet, very interesting to see the war from the perspective of the Vietnamese. The strong feelings continued as we stepped outside into a display of captured US antiaircraft weapons, missiles, tanks, trucks, cannon, jeeps, and armament. In the midst of all this was the wreckage of a B-52 bomber. What made this all bearable was the fact that I never did see the museum guides, personnel, or visitors gloat over these displays. They were respectful and looked at me with sadness in their eyes, hope for the future, and the look of "Why did this have to happen?" I shared their feelings.

Roy walked me across the street and made me pose in front of the statue of V.I. Lenin, perhaps the only statue of Lenin still displayed in the world today, since other Lenin monuments have been torn down or destroyed. (While traveling in Russia in the summer of 1995 we did see a Lenin statue in Moscow.) This particular sculpture is large, impressive, and of the stereotypical variety that was dedicated in Hanoi by Mikhail Gorbachev from the USSR on one of his visits to this capital.

Roy and I hurried to his car and the driver took Roy to his office, running the constant gauntlet of bicycles, motorbikes, and cyclos. Surely, we would run over someone today. How could we miss in this scrambled maze of traveling humanity? With UN flag flying and my smiling while holding my breath, we reached UNDP headquarters. Roy rushed to his office after instructing the driver to deliver me to his residence and return immediately. I promptly moved over to the rear right seat. The driver drove to the UNDP gate, got out of the car, and covered the UN flag, as I slumped forward with a scowl on my face. Oh well, at least I had a car and driver.

Back at the residence, Delores announced there would be no rest nor massage this afternoon, because Linda and she had decided we were going shopping for souvenirs for our children and families back in Phoenix and Tucson. Three of our four children are married and have produced six precious grandchildren, ages four through eight, for us. In addition to these 13 family members, we also needed to think of something meaningful to take to Linda's mom and my mom. I proposed "Good Morning, Vietnam" t-shirts, but Linda wasn't keen on the idea and opted for Delores to direct her driver to take us to the silver block, to purchase silver engraved boxes, bottles, and figurines. Linda forced herself to go to the city street to buy items of silk: kimonos, pajamas, shirts, and blouses. All were inexpensive, $4 to $12., and of good quality. The clerks were friendly and fair, but puzzled by our multiple purchases. They offered, and we accepted on this humid day, what else, a can of Coca Cola. I still managed to purchase the t-shirts.

After a long, productive, and interesting day, we came back to the residence, dressed, and prepared for a special event. The invitation received at the residence prior to our arrival stated:

The Ambassador

of the Republic of Indonesia and Mrs. Juwana

request the pleasure of the company of

Dr. Roy D. Morey, and Madam

and Guests, Dr. Charles D. Pilon and Madam

at Reception

on Friday, 18 February at 18:30 hours

at NgH8 Njo Qnyen Street

Regrets Only

To Bid Farewell

We rode in the rain in Roy's staff car, flag flying. Almost every car at the Indonesian Embassy had a flag flying. I was in flag heaven. While at the reception, Roy and Delores presented Linda and me to the Ambassador and Madame from Indonesia. Then we were introduced to ambassadors from Italy, Germany, United Kingdom, Canada, Finland, etc. We also met several business people from Sweden, India, Canada, and Australia. Even General Vinh, the Director of International Relations Ministry of Defense, was pointed out to us.

We listened to all the farewell speeches and toasts, while we sampled the food and punch before bidding Ambassador and Madam Jawana our best as they leave the ambassador post in Vietnam and go to their new assignment in Beijing, China. Ambassador and Mrs. Jawana were most gracious, as we wished them well in their new position and told them how much we hoped they would find China to their liking, even though it's very different from Vietnam. Seemingly genuine, they kindly asked us to consider visiting them there. We felt very honored by their attention, especially understanding their overwhelming duties at such an affair. Sometimes, it really does happen that, the higher position one attains, the more gracious one becomes. I have a hunch that this particular couple were charming people long before this particular evening.

The driver whisked us back to the residence, and we were served a late, sumptuous dinner with some more fine Morey wine. We went to bed immediately after dinner, as there would be an early departure of 7:00 A.M. scheduled for the next day's venture.

Dr. Hoang Duc Nhuan, Director General,
National Institute for Educational Science of Vietnam

Lt. Alvarez, USN - first American Pilot captured in Vietnam War

60

NAU Commemorative Plate presented to Dr. Truyen by Chuck

Chuck meeting with Vietnam Ministry of Education

61

Hanoi Street Scene

Sidewalk Barber Shop - Hanoi

# Chapter Four

# VIETNAM CASUALTY

The anticipation of this day's outing and the excitement I was feeling just hearing about what we were going to experience provided mixed emotions. We had been only slightly briefed about what to expect on our trip to a very holy and remote site, the Perfume Pagoda.

We were up at 6:00 A.M. on Saturday and were met at the residence by two vans and drivers at 7:00 A.M. One van was loaded with a guide/interpreter, Roy, Delores, Linda, me, and the driver. The second one had Vietnamese government officials, guides, and their family members. We sped out of Hanoi dodging, swerving, honking the horn, and playing "chicken" with the thousands upon thousands of bicycles, motorbikes, cyclos, and pedestrians. Both vans headed northwest, passing the Vietnam Air Museum, B-52 Park and B-52 Boulevard. Before long we were into the country and traveling through village after village. Soon, beautiful mountains with a morning mist enveloping them, mysteriously appeared on the horizon. It made me think we were wandering into the Vietnamese version of Brigadoon. By now we were traveling through rich farm land with thriving rice paddies and the ever-present water buffalo, tended by the young boy of the family, doing his duty. We saw more than one duck herder, traveling with his large flock along this rural road or crossing the dikes between fields. I knew I was in the jungle of Vietnam when the road narrowed, there were fewer villages, and the sights of papaya and banana trees were prevalent. We had traveled about two hours without stopping, when we began following a river and soon came to a guarded bridge with many festive Vietnamese crossing it. Our two vans were ordered to stop by the soldier/police. I saw smiles on these military faces when they looked into the vehicles, especially into ours. I felt like a dollar sign. It was soon obvious that there had to be a payment of either US dollars or dong or both. The only argument now was how much. A negotiated fee was accepted, and the barrier was lifted for us to cross the river on a very narrow and crude bridge that didn't look like it would hold our heavy-laden vans. We entered what seemed to be the most remote village that I could imagine to have existed in Vietnam; yet, it was teeming with people. Located on the river, its biggest concession was the countless number of rental boats that covered the waterway, bank to bank, for several hundred yards. A new negotiating round began. This time the fee was for a large boat, able to carry the thirteen of us upstream and back from the pagoda. First, there had to be a time-out so all of us could relieve ourselves, after that long and harrowing ride. One of the Vietnamese men accompanying us looked at me and asked, "You must pee pee?"

I said, "Oh yes, yes, oh yes." He led me across the road into

64

the private quarters of a Vietnamese family. I walked into and through a combination kitchen with noodles simmering and tea brewing, parlor where men and boys were smoking, and bedroom where an old woman and baby were sleeping. Some dishes in a tin can were in the process of being washed. Clothes were being laundered in another metal container. I was led into the concrete stall with no covering on the open doorway. Climbing up to the top step, I refused to continue down to the next or bottom level into the stall. There was a concrete drain leading from the stall to the outside. I prepared to relieve myself and looked over my right shoulder, and, just as I had sensed, there stood two little old women, two young male teenagers, and several children, watching this phenomenon. Yes, I am sure they surmised, Americans urinate like we do. By this time, I cared less if I was the sight of the day. I hurried as fast as I could, but I am never very good with an audience. I held my breath all the time, because the stench of decades of urine was as strong as any odor I have ever experienced. As I zipped up, an old lady grabbed my arm and asked, "You want wash?" So she wouldn't think Americans were uncouth, I let her splash some dish water on my hands before I dried them with a rag hanging from the concrete wall. Now, I really did need to wash my hands. Hurrying across the road, I was directed to a large metal boat that looked like it had been molded and welded from large steel drum containers, the kind I used to see in my dad's Texaco station, back in Scottsdale, Arizona. Linda, Roy, and Delores sat behind me on one of three

65

wooden planks mounted in the boat for seats. I sat with a Vietnamese couple. Their eight year old son sat on a picnic box. He looked like a four year old and certainly wasn't as large as our eight year old grandson, Chase. (All the Vietnamese appear to be younger and are smaller than the average American.) There were two crewmen working each boat: one fore, paddling at a steady pace, another aft, paddling just as vigorously, but also steering the boat. Once settled into the boat with my trusty little camera in the ready position, I looked upstream and saw what I thought was the end of the river. I estimated the sight of the river visible to me to be about two miles. As we reached what I thought was our destination, the river turned, then ran around a mountain and curved around a village. The boats traveled on the river over an hour through jungle, past some rice paddies, and even stopped at a river pagoda to pay a toll fee in order to proceed to our destination. We were reconciled to this routine of travel and greatly enjoyed the whole panorama of river, mountains on the horizon, wild birds, banana, coconut, papaya, and mango trees. I was busy taking many pictures of the beautiful terrain as well as the tremendous river traffic. Suddenly there was a yell and a splash. I jerked around and saw a Vietnamese army helmet floating in the water. Everyone scrambled, and up came one of our boatmen. The hemp holding his oar had worn through, and the break caused him to topple into the lily padded water. Someone grabbed his helmet, and another put out a hand and helped him back aboard the boat. No one was hurt, but the boatman was wet and slightly embarrassed. Staring at him, I decided not to use my camera, and the boatman smiled at me for the first time that day. I smiled back, and the ice was broken. He appeared friendly after that. All the other Vietnamese on the river laughed as they witnessed our little mishap. The boats going in our direction traveled close to us for a stretch, before racing off to beat the Americans to the destination. All seemed curious but cautious, as they moved with us, then past us. People in boats moving in the opposite direction going back to the village, all smiled and waved. As we all were thoroughly enjoying this jungle scenery, I heard, "Hey U.S." I turned and looked behind me at a boat loaded with young Vietnamese teenage couples. They were all smoking and held up their Coke cans, proudly displaying them to us. The girls were wearing denim jackets and lots of costume jewelry. The boys had on jeans and wild and crazy Hawaiian style shirts. Certainly not looking like the teens of the villages through which we had traveled, these had to be of the new city generation of Hanoi. Noticing my camera, one of them said, "Take picture." I dutifully did. Then they tauntingly embraced and repeated, "Now, take picture." I again complied. They came closer to our boat and offered me a cigarette. I politely refuse by saying, "I, no smoke." They laughed hilariously. As they taunted me, one young man took off his wrist watch, saying, "Trade?" Smiling, I shook my head. Then he eyed my class ring and took off one of his own rings and said, "Ring, trade?" Again, I politely demurred. This teenage boater continued paddling alongside for at least a mile. They continued to

67

smoke, hug their girl friends and tease me about trading articles, always asking for their picture to be taken. Most everyone had by now tired of these somewhat pesky young teenagers. I continued to watch them with amusement. As I tired of their teasing and exchange, I finally looked away. The leader of their group then said in a normal tone, "Hey U.S." As I turned, he made a typically teenage gesture of disrespect, pointing his middle finger in an upward direction toward me, and mouthed, "Fuck you, U.S." That was the first and last negative gesture/comment that I personally witnessed in all our stay in Vietnam. I still think he was teasing, practicing his English, and just being a wise guy. I chalked up the experience and remarked to the embarrassed Vietnamese interpreter who had also noted this little exchange, "Teenagers seem to be the same the world over. We have some of this variety back in Arizona."

Finally, after what seemed like half the day, I saw dozens and dozens of boats anchored several hundred yards ahead. Large colorful silk flags were flying from many staffs. Vendors were selling fresh fruit, cool Coca Cola, Buddhist religious articles, crafts, canes, walking sticks, and even rolls of film from the many bamboo huts in the docking area. Here also is where the beginning of the trail to the Perfume Pagoda began. About a hundred yards ahead, I could see the structures of ancient Buddhist monasteries, statues of Buddha, and statues of animals, interspersed between mango and papaya trees. There were literally thousands of people walking the trail. I thought, "Hey, this is a piece of cake. We walk up the path a few hundred yards, and we are at our destination." I couldn't have been more wrong.

Along the way, we passed a continuous line of little booths, with vendors constantly hawking their products. There were even stalls that served as sleeping quarters that could be rented for the night if one chose to stay overnight. The beds in these booths were merely pieces of plywood on stilts, with bamboo mats on top. Many people were negotiating for their lodging. We finally reached the monastery, and I was so pleased to take a break. I vigorously began snapping pictures of temples, statues, papaya trees, people, monks, and our party. One of the guides strolled up and asked, "You pee pee now, please?"

I thought, great. Just what I need before I proceed with my photography. I was led to this solid structure and through its gate. The path led into a courtyard with open stalls and concrete slits on the ground. The stench again, was horrible. I held my breath as long as I could, then groaned on exhale and held my breath again. On the third groan, I heard Delores ask, "You okay, Chuck?"

I turned as I instantly realized this was a unisex toilet. My muscles immediately went into the stop mode, and I couldn't finish. I ran out, and we both laughed, as I rushed off to alert Linda to the pee pee stop.

Our party was then formally introduced to the head Buddhist monk, the most revered religious man in residence. He was very gracious, warmly wished us well, and told us that a formal meal would be served to us later in the day. I was puzzled and asked, "Why don't we just eat now?" I was told that this monastery was not our destination. This was not the Perfume Pagoda. The most holy Perfume Pagoda was over two miles away, straight up the mountain. I thought briefly about not going, but immediately realized that was an impossibility. To not go would be the ultimate insult to these Vietnamese who were so proud to show their most holy sight to us Americans.

There had been steady rain the previous day and night, causing the rocky trail to be slippery with mud. It normally would have been a beautiful hike through the heavy jungle along the mountain ridge line, but all concentration was focused on maintaining equilibrium with every step, rather than enjoying the lush scenery. My lungs kept reminding me of the steep grade we were climbing. I had to stop often to catch my breath. I wanted an ice cold coke bad, but didn't stop to buy one, because I knew I didn't want to cope with the carbonation during this ordeal. All devout Buddhists in the area are expected to make the journey to the Perfume Pagoda annually. Mr. Hieu, who was our chief guide, makes this religious pilgrimage several times a year. The thousands of Vietnamese people making the pilgrimage to their holy shrine just after this Tet season, were something to behold. All of them stared at us and cleared the way for us. When I stopped to catch my breath, the pilgrims would smile, giggle, or wish us luck. They all motioned us with voice and hand signals to greet each other with "A di da phat.", meaning, ask Buddha to safely guide and bless us on our journey. As I stopped, I noticed the wonderfully pious attitude these men, women, children, teens, old, lame, and religious displayed as they trudged on to their destination. Most of these people carried offerings of fruit, vegetables, drinks, meat, fish, religious medallions, incense sticks, and money to their Buddha. The piety on the faces of the people coming back down the mountain was even more evident.      During one of my rest stops, I realized that I was covered with red mud from my knees down to my New Balance tennis shoes. I was sweating so profusely from the extra exertion as well as the humidity, that I was completely soaked. Little old ladies wearing sandals with no mud on them were passing me. Vietnamese men in suits, ties, and dress shoes, appeared to be untouched by the mud. I couldn't understand how these people could so easily climb this trail with oddly dysfunctional footwear, formal clothing, and carrying heavy packages of offerings. I was wearing the latest in American sport shoes, comfortable, casual clothing, and carrying absolutely nothing. I thought maybe one had to be a Buddhist.

Linda chose to walk with me and a Vietnamese interpreter/pilgrim. Roy and Delores are better hikers and were out in front and constantly waiting for us. Finally we reached the site of the Perfume Pagoda, only to see that now we had to walk a steep 700 plus steps down into a giant cave in the mountain, where the Buddha had been placed. Looking into the cave, Delores, Linda, and I could barely make out the Buddha, due to the dense smoke from thousands of prayer sticks that had been lit. Roy was already into the cave. His long legs, strong lungs, and extreme curiosity, put him at the head of our party. We other three agreed, okay we've seen it, we don't need to climb down into that smoke-filled cave. Immediately we had second thoughts and knew we had to go down into the cave, because we were here. It was expected, and we had to be courteous and diplomatic. Off we went. As we alighted from the last of a very long flight of steps, our guide motioned us to proceed first to the front of the Buddha, then behind it to the very back of the cave. He offered us Coca Cola, cold from the temperature of the cave, as well as oranges, tangerines, and bananas. The coke was the most welcome and delicious drink imaginable.

After our Vietnamese friends prayed and paid homage, we retraced our journey by climbing those 700 or so steps back up to the entrance of the cave. Then, we took a well-deserved rest and thought about the easy walk down the two plus mile mountain trail to an eagerly anticipated meal with the revered chief Buddhist monk and official UNDP party. The trail was like ice because the clay-like mud had been pounded by the many thousands of feet tromping over it. We were all repeatedly warned to watch our steps. Bamboo walking sticks were offered to all in our party. Only Linda decided she would feel more secure with a bamboo pole, as we trudged down this glassy trail. Mr. Hieu, one of the Vietnamese gentlemen, insisted on holding Linda's hand, so she wouldn't fall. She constantly slipped and clutched both the pole and his hand. I was walking down at a good but lackadaisical pace, slipping and sliding, while both Mr. Hieu and Linda cautioned me to be careful. All of a sudden I stepped on a smooth rock hidden just under the surface of the mud, lost my footing, and flew several feet down the muddy trail, sliding and tumbling. I knew I was hurt, but I couldn't stop my quick descent. I finally grabbed a rock and stopped. I lay there on the trail out of breath, bleeding from knee, elbow, and hand, and wondering what had happened. Linda and Mr. Hieu finally reached me, and with the aid of several Vietnamese men and women on the trail, helped me up. I was assisted to an overnight accommodation booth. That little episode of the out-of-breath American tumbling down the mountain trail drew Vietnamese pilgrim gasps, ohs, ahs, screams, shouting, and even laughter. Immediately, people began wiping the mud off me with newspapers, tissues, cloths, and leaves. One man gave me a drink of his water. A lady wiped my face. Linda frantically tried to see my right knee through my torn and bloody pant leg. She surprised me by coolly grabbing the torn pants at the knee and ripping them open. That was the exact move I had been taught when I was an Air Force medic. She then wiped as much blood and mud off my knee as possible with such limited means. She claims I was in shock. Actually, I was in shock at all the attention I was getting from total strangers. They were all very concerned and worried about the clumsy American. One man stopped and emptied his water bottle to wash out the wound. Another stopped and opened a miniature whiskey bottle and emptied it on my knee to disinfect it. Mr. Hieu was busy borrowing paper, tissue, and cloth to clean the wound. One lady shoved two white pills into my hand with a bottle of water to get them down. She looked at me and said, "You take, you take, now, you take." I dutifully obeyed my caretaker and swallowed the little white pills.

Linda excitedly asked, "Chuck, what did you just take?"

I answered, "I don't know. She said take and I took them."

Linda, with eyes bigger than normal, grabbed my arm and said, "My God, what if it was penicillin?" I almost fainted then. I thought, Oh shit, I barely made it out of my last reaction to this antibiotic several years ago. Wouldn't that be the shits if I had mistakenly taken penicillin, to which I'm allergic, and got a bad reaction here on this remote mountain trail in Vietnam? Linda frantically tried to ask the kind lady, "Were those pills, penicillin? You know penicillin? Medicine, penicillin."

The only answer the smiling lady gave was, "Good, good, good medicine. Yes, good, good, good." I thought too late now, and anyway it hasn't hit yes, so I must be home free. The last penicillin reaction had begun within minutes.

Another lady stopped and offered her scissors and cut off my pant leg at mid thigh. Then she dug into her bag and produced an army bandage, which she skillfully wrapped around my knee, after another man put the finishing touches on the dressing by emptying two small bottles of what appeared to be a wintergreen solution. It felt cool and soothing. After my knee was wrapped, Mr. Hieu began to rub the bandaged wound and pray a Buddhist chant for my healing and recovery. He kept asking me if I felt better, and I said, yes. And, I really did. Mr. Hieu would not let me move or stand until he finished his prayers and recited a second round. It was good to sit, relax, and regain my composure, as I evaluated the situation. I had a gash on my left hand and scratches on my right elbow, plus the cut knee. I was pretty sore and very embarrassed. Every single Vietnamese stopped to stare at me in curiosity. As Mr. Hieu assisted me to my feet, I shook the cobwebs from my head and noticed a teenager, who curiously, irritated me. He mustered his best English to graphically point at me and say, "Heepee." I looked at my one cut-off pant leg, exposing the olive drab bandage around my knee and admitted, "Yes, hippie." He laughed, shook his head, waved his hand at me, signalling, "You crazy American." If I had implored Buddha with, "a di da phat," maybe I wouldn't have found myself in this embarrassing situation.

Mr. Hieu grabbed my left hand in his and said, "I hold your hand to bottom."

I said, "No, that's okay. I am all right."

Mr. Hieu replied, "I hold your hand and my strength will flow to you. I will pray for you all way down. You be stronger and be better with good spirit."

I couldn't get out of it, so we descended the mountain trail, my hand in Mr. Hieu's. I was limping, covered with mud, a bandage on my knee, and one missing pant leg. I was a sight for all. I was quite the celebrity, making a fool of myself, but entertaining all who saw me. The news about me had preceded me down the mountain, and people were waiting to see this oddity. They stood aside and either giggled or sympathized with me as I passed.

In the meantime, Roy and Delores were over half way down, wondering what the hell happened to Chuck and Linda. One man who had seen me fall and go through all the first aid ministrations, walked up to Roy and asked, "You wait for your American friend?"

Roy replied, "Yes, I wait for my American friend."

The Vietnamese man said, "Your friend, he break he knee."

Roy and Delores frantically looked at each other. Roy thought, "Oh no. Chuck's whole mission to Vietnam is over. I have to figure out a way to rig some kind of litter and carry him down the mountain, cancel our wonderful meal with the Buddhist monk, move Chuck as rapidly as possible down the river to the village, speed quickly down the rural roads of the jungle to locate a phone and call for a helicopter to take him to Hanoi, where he can then be transported to Bangkok for anticipated treatment." Roy reached me in record time with Delores close behind.

Excitedly he asked, "Chuck, what happened? You okay?" He then related his frantic thoughts. We stopped and laughed, realizing that when the Vietnamese said, "broke knee," he meant the skin of the knee was broken. Relieved, Roy began his teasing. At one point I asked Mr. Hieu what a certain important-looking sign said. Roy immediately blurted out, "It says, Yankee go home."

Mr. Hieu got all excited and said, "Oh no, no, no, not say, Yankee go home. Mr. Roy make a joke."

Roy said, "Look, Mr. Hieu, I read Vietnamese. That is exactly what that sign says, Chuck. Yankee go home." Roy winked at me and watched Mr. Hieu almost go ballistic.

Hieu said, "Oh no, please no, no, please. Not say go home. Mr. Roy so funny, very funny. You make joke, Mr. Roy." Roy never answered and continued walking ahead. I assured Mr. Hieu that Dr. Morey was a famous jokester who made funnies. I explained that I had known Roy for almost forty years, and knew he was only kidding. Mr. Hieu seemed so relieved. He then continued to pray and transfer all that energy to me. It worked, because we all made it down that slippery mud trail. We even stopped to experience the cool winds blowing through the canyons and enjoyed the sights of gorgeous land in the distance. I thought how peaceful this part of Vietnam was. Perhaps it always has been, this remote piece of paradise with a pious legacy of peace, prayers, and tranquility. This is the way all holy places should be, untouched by war or conflict of any kind, only an occasional spill is permissible.

Word had preceded me to the monastery. People, waving and laughing, were waiting to see me. The head of the monks greeted us and warmly shook our hands. He even took Linda's and Delores' hands as he greeted them. (This was very unusual, as Buddhist monks are very careful never to touch women. Females make sure they move back, so as not to accidentally brush against a monk.) He looked at me, smiled, grabbed both my hands in his, and chanted some prayers. I was very honored. He then led us to a private reception room, where we were seated and served a delicious Vietnamese lunch, followed by watermelon, oranges, bananas, and lotus blossom seeds. The chief and most holy monk presented us with religious medallions he placed around our necks and gave us red envelopes with dong inside. This was his New Year, or Tet, present to us, following the Buddhist custom. He posed for pictures and blessed us, bidding us a safe journey on the boats to the village, and back to Hanoi. He said we were always welcome and to please return.

The ride back down the river to the village was just as impressive and pretty as going up. We stopped at the same Buddhist Shrine on our way back to pay a toll and allow the men to pee on the fence a few feet from the boat. The men of Vietnam have no qualms about relieving themselves in public. They can be walking down the street, and when the urge hits, they look for a wall, and urinate there. It is amazing to be travelling or walking and see the men just stop and "let fly." American men will also do the same thing, only they are discreet and hide where they think no one will see them. I did not see any women do this on the streets. They are like American men. They hide and block themselves from public view before they relieve themselves. The peasant Vietnamese women; however, just squat in the fields, on the dikes, or in the water and relieve themselves. A UNDP staff member told me that they have serious gynecological problems because the women do this in such unsanitary places as the rice paddies.

We continued down the waterway seeing hundreds and hundreds of ducks crossing the river at one time. Upon reaching the village, we again borrowed the facilities of another village family, and these people also stood and watched me urinate in their concrete trough, just off the kitchen. I attracted more attention because I was missing one pant leg. By now the blood had begun to show through the bandage, and a little had flowed down my leg. The story of the wounded American had preceded me to the village, and people were lined up to see this funny lame guy with one pant leg. Again, half the villagers laughed at me and half stared in sympathy. All waved as we drove away headed for the "tall" bridge. On the way out we were hailed by the merchants, selling plucked ducks, plucked chickens, gutted out pigs, and skinned dogs. Vendors of vegetables, fruits, and drinks beckoned to us. We again paid our fee to cross the bridge, onto a very basic dirt road through jungles, then rice paddies, back to Hanoi. We passed both Buddhist pagodas and Catholic churches and saw Buddhist and Catholic cemeteries. We even passed through the fireworks village, where the majority of fireworks for celebrating Tet and other special occasions, are produced. We also went through hundreds upon hundreds of banana, papaya, and mango groves.

The road was very rough and bumpy. There was barely enough light to drive without headlights. I was hoping we could reach Hanoi in daylight or at least get out of the jungle before nightfall. I didn't feel comfortable so far from the city with evening approaching. The country was absolutely beautiful during the day, but in the dark, it gave me bad vibes. (EERIE.) I was more comfortable once we reached the outskirts of Hanoi and could see the teeming population again on bicycles, motorbikes, and cyclos. It was Saturday night, and the crowds were out on the streets. We reached the Morey residence and I immediately took off my tennis shoes and hosed off the few pounds of mud they had collected. I waited for the vans to leave, then emptied my pants' pockets and took off my pants to be discarded. I evaluated my muddy torn shirt and also took it off. Carefully noting my limping, Delores and Linda followed me into the residence. I was clad only in my jockey shorts. I stopped at the door and put on my slippers and started up the stairs. Linda, Delores, and Roy watched and laughed, as I headed for the shower and clean dressings for my knee. I stopped on the stairs, looked down at this laughing trio and reminded them that we needed to stop this kind of dress behavior. That statement took us all back several years to a camping vacation in Pennsylvania, when Roy and I were drenched, changing a broken spring on his camping trailer in a downpour. Because we had been so wet and cold, we had stripped down to our underwear to continue our trip of several more hours to get to our camping site in the Shenandoahs. We have laughed about this experience many times, but it was pretty miserable at the time.

After an all-day journey in the wilds of Vietnam, I was about to take a good hot shower, survey my wound, and rebandage it. I unwrapped the army dressing carefully and broke the beginning healing process by starting the bleeding again. By all rights, I should have had about five or six sutures in my knee, but I endured. The shower and new dressing felt great, and I appeared for dinner in pajamas and robe. The Morey's cook outdid himself this evening, and I was very hungry. The wine even tasted better. There wasn't a lot of time spent over coffee in the living room that night. We were all tired but contented. Roy teased me, "Leave it to you, Chuck, to attract so much attention. They loved it."

I countered with, "Oh yeah, Mr. Roy, you always make funny joke."

Off to bed to rest up for another adventure the next day. There was no giggling in bed that night. The knee had become pretty sore and swollen. It didn't help that it was the same old knee that had been injured playing college football many years ago.

Rental boats awaiting travelers to the Perfume Pagoda

Bargaining for boat rentals

Boatman
Roy, Delores, Linda

River Trip to Temple and Perfume Pagoda

Path to Perfume Pagoda

Perfume Pagoda Cave

Chuck, Linda, and Mr. Hieu,
after Chuck's fall on the trail

Temple at base of mountain where Perfume
Pagoda is located

# Chapter Five

# BAT BAT

The day began perfectly when for breakfast I was served the largest papaya I have ever seen. The only explanation I have for the extra large papayas grown in Vietnam is perhaps the use of "honey buckets" (human wastes), for fertilizer. We were met by Loan, a Vietnamese friend of the Moreys, who would act as our interpreter, guide, and hostess for today's excursion. Before leaving Hanoi, we had to stop one more time to take photographs of the Ho Chi Minh Mausoleum, the Palace of Government, the Communist Party Headquarters, and other government buildings in the vicinity. As soon as we arrived in the countryside, I decided the entire area was a photographer's utopia. There were scenes of farmers planting rice crops in their fields. Water buffalo were in the fields, tended by their young masters. We saw dozens of flocks of ducks. Their herders kept them in line, guiding them by means of long bamboo poles with plastic bags tied on the ends. There were also scenes of clever irrigators, holding hemp handles with a large water tin tied to the middle. In unison the paired handlers would maneuver the bucket into the stream to be filled with water; then, with perfect wrist action and timing, flip the water from the bucket into the field, and on the back swing, refill the bucket, to again water the field.  Not a beat was missed, and no water spilled where it shouldn't have.  This was real athletic skill and coordination.  I would award them all a perfect score of 10 for their performance.  They went through this routine for hours.  What perseverance, but so necessary where machine run pumps were not affordable.

The bright sun brought out the brilliant greens of the rice fields, as they were tended by the black clad peasants in their conical straw hats.  This hard working rural society performs their chores from sun-up till past sundown, seven days a week, three- hundred-sixty-five days a year.

Loan asked if we wanted to see an old French Catholic church.  In the middle of the densely overgrown jungle was a steeple with a large cross sticking up above the tree tops.  This particular church had been built for members of the French army in 1950, as there had been a large French military garrison stationed nearby.  We drove as close as we could to it and noticed a small replica of the famous Lourdes Grotto in France.

Loan knocked on the gate to see if the local priest would come to greet us.  As we grew impatient and started to walk away, a very small ancient-looking Vietnamese Catholic priest opened the gate and smiled.  Loan introduced herself and informed him of the four American visitors who would like to see the church, which was padlocked.  He unlocked the door and welcomed us into the Church of Notre Dame.  The floor was inlaid stone, and must have been magnificent in its day. Most of the old wooden pews and kneelers were warped, broken, or missing. There was a small puddle of water under the once impressive high and massive dome. I noticed some broken stained glass in the dome and a large crack in the concrete cupola. I requested Loan to ask the priest what happened. When I heard the answer, "B-52.", I understood. I thought how terribly ironic. There may have been U. S. Catholic pilots bombing one of their churches. I walked down the center aisle and approached the main altar, dedicated to Jesus Christ. The main side altars honored the Blessed Virgin Mary and St. Francis of Assisi. Minor side altars were devoted to St. Theresa and Joan of Arc. I noticed a large, faded, and scarred picture of the Pope John Paul II hung over a falling-down pulpit. It was Sunday, and I asked the priest if there were a mass today. He said he was eighty-eight years old and he only has the strength to say mass a few times a month. Then leading us into a once-beautiful courtyard and orchard, now overgrown and run-down, he pointed out the remains of a former seminary and convent, plus school. We asked if there were restrooms. He first led the men through a walkway into an open garden area. He motioned us forward. We saw only a barbed wire fence surrounding a vacant field. I wondered how the ladies were going to react to these facilities but thought this was certainly a more pleasant situation than what we had encountered the previous day on our trip to the Perfume Pagoda.

As we walked toward the van, about fifteen little children suddenly appeared from the dense vegetation, approaching us timidly. We all smiled and said hello. They yelled almost in unison, "Hal-low, hal-low, hal-low." I positioned my camera for a photograph, and they immediately scattered. I put away the camera, and they reappeared. I reached for the camera, and they vanished. This routine was repeated several times. Needless to say, I never did get a picture of the children. As the van was driven away, the children ran following us, singing out, "Hal-low," and waved till we disappeared.

We then drove to the vicinity of Bat Bat and tried to locate the site where the American pilots imprisoned in the "Hanoi Hilton" were eventually relocated, when the bombing in Hanoi increased. Rumor had it that the U.S. had planned a daring rescue mission of the U.S. pilots at Bat Bat, but Hanoi intelligence detected this, and the prisoners were moved again to a still top-secret location.

As we were driving through the village of Bat Bat, we all remarked, what a beautiful location for a picnic. Loan and the driver had quite a discussion, as we stopped in front of a two-story dwelling on the edge of a papaya grove. There was a short conversation with the occupants of the house, and we found ourselves climbing the outside staircase to the roof. The driver, brought out a bamboo mat and spread it on the rooftop deck, which overlooked a lake. Loan, who had brought lunch, opened the picnic basket and began peeling a very large, fresh papaya, which she served us sprinkled with lime.

Next, came the home-made potato chips, rice, miniature bananas, nam (spring rolls), and chicken, accompanied by Canada Dry ginger ale. The neighborhood children kept sneaking up the stairs to gawk at us. When they saw us eating the papaya, they immediately began bringing several more papaya, fresh from the grove. Soon we had more papaya than we could possibly eat in a week, so we had to beg and bribe them to stop bringing them. The begging didn't work, but the bribes did. They very clearly understood dong. After our delicious meal and photos all around, we gave the occupants of the home some money and left. All the while we joked that when we next looked for a picnic spot while camping in the United States, we would try to select a home with a lovely patio or deck, preferably one with a nice view, and then negotiate a price with the owners, so we could have our picnic there.

Loan decided to give us all a treat by inviting us to the village of her childhood, which was on the way back to Hanoi. She mentioned that her mother had her teeth lacquered black when she was a young woman, and perhaps we would like to see this phenomenon. It was exciting to be given such an opportunity. We had to park outside the village and walk in, because no automobiles were allowed, or could fit on the small dirt lanes, for that matter. As we walked down the narrow path, we were a curious sight to all the villagers, especially the children. We may have been the first Americans they had seen in the village. Loan led us into her mother's house and proudly pointed to an outside water pump. The

89

last time I had seen one of those in use was at Linda's parent's remote forest cabin in Payson, Arizona, some thirty years before. Loan had this pump installed to help make her mother's life easier. Another thing Loan did for her mother was buy her an exotic miniature Chinese breed puppy. It was cute and only a few months old but had already been bred, so Loan's mother could sell the expected puppies for a nice fee, to supplement her income. Everyone's attention was occupied by the puppy, until it wet the straw mat that Loan's mother used for a bed. After some spirited conversation, we saw the water pump in action as the bamboo mat was cleaned.

Relying on her daughter as the interpreter, Loan's mother asked us to please sit down and have some tea. We seated ourselves in the kitchen/living area of the two-room home, and Loan served us the typical green tea in miniature cups, which she pre-warmed by pouring boiling water in them. We were surprised to see a television set in this very basic home without indoor plumbing nor running water. There was, however, a predominantly displayed large picture of a nice looking man, whom we presumed to be Loan's deceased father. It is typical to enshrine deceased members of the family, especially parents.

Loan asked us if we would like to see her mother's church. Her mother is Catholic, as many of her friends are. It is almost a social outlet for her. As we approached the church, we drew an overwhelming crowd of children and teens, who almost knocked us over with their excited exuberance. We entered the church, which was packed with parishioners devoutly praying the rosary in sing-song unison. I wished I had a tape recorder. It sounded beautifully reverent. I honored their piety and did not take photographs, but the subject was perfect for it. There was a marked absence in the church of young people. All those wrinkled-up, tiny, elderly people were kneeling in their pews with their homemade and varied conglomeration of rosaries, reciting so devoutly the litany in perfect and loud unison. It was a small, beautifully kept, clean church, which reminded me of Our Lady of Guadalupe Catholic Church, in Flagstaff, Arizona. There, on any given day, especially during mariachi masses, little old Hispanic ladies and men pray in unison, exhibiting profound devotion. It is a rich and inspirational experience, regardless of one's own religion or ethnic persuasion.

We took our share of photos of the outside of the church, the less-shy children, and the oldest man of the village. He looked 101. I don't know what his age was, but he was a perfect double for Ho Chi Minh, himself.

Loan's mother proudly posed for pictures with all of us in her garden of beautiful, homegrown carnations. She could not smile enough for us, showing off her jet black lacquered teeth. Loan told us her mother had the procedure done when she was very young. It had been painful, and her mouth was sore and swollen for a long time. It was believed that the lacquer was attractive as well as protective, making her teeth strong. It had been the fashionable thing for young ladies of her generation to do. The option was either red or black. Loan's mother chose black because it was more sophisticated and beautiful. The practice became unpopular when the French disapproved, so today only the older ladies have lacquered teeth.

I noticed the cornerstone of the church had the year, "1899," commemorating its founding date. That was easy for me to remember, since it's also the year Northern Arizona University was founded as Northern Arizona Normal School.

As we walked out of the village where the USA had some wonderful good-will ambassadors at work, we bade goodbye to Loan's mother. I remarked to Loan that her mother reminded me of my own grandmothers, but I quickly kept quiet when I learned that her mother was only a few years older than I am.

Upon returning to Hanoi, we stopped at the diplomatic housing compound to see Loan's little business venture. Much to our surprise, Loan proudly showed us the small convenience store/cafe that she operates, and is located in the main building of the compound. We purchased several bottles of Vietnamese chili sauce, for our son-in-law Kelly Mero, who loves hot chili. We didn't find anything else distinctively Vietnamese. Our choices were Campbell soups, French's mustard, Coca Cola, Tabasco sauce, Skippy peanut butter, Del Monte peaches, etc. As the customers strolled in for their items, they seemed very pleased with the selection of products as well as the prices. Loan was offering a most appreciated service and helping herself and family by earning extra income as well as providing jobs for her relatives.

Back at the residence we relived the day over our favorite dinner, homemade New Mexican style green chile enchiladas prepared by Delores and Linda. Roy contributed with that delicious San Miguel beer from the Philippines. Roy and Delores hoard these green chile enchilada meals, so we were honored to be sharing such prized food and also slipping back into our summer camping traditions of these enchiladas for most meals. (We will do the same this summer.)

Another day, another adventure. I was so fulfilled that night that I did not even hear the constant jingling of cyclo and bicycle bells, the ever-present automobile horn-honking, nor the frighteningly loud fire crackers going off all through the night in perpetual celebration of Tet.

Plowing with water buffalo

Notre Dame Church built for French soldiers in 1950

Loan, Priest, Roy, Chuck, Linda, our Driver

Herding the water buffalo

Picnic on the Roof - Loan, Delores, Roy, Linda

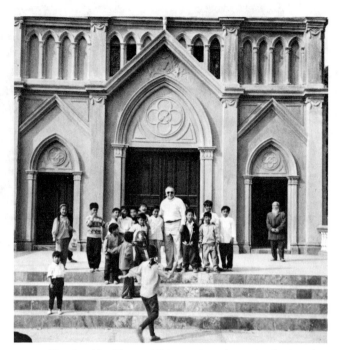

Chuck with village children - Loan's mother's church

Chuck, Village Elder, Roy

# Chapter Six

# THE MOUNTAIN CAMPUS

I could get used to waking up in the Morey's home in Hanoi every morning, and having a breakfast of the delicious, giant papaya, French bread, and coffee as we listened to the "Voice of America" broadcast on Roy and Delores' shortwave radio. This day's official duties would take me to the Viet Bac Teacher Training College, north of Hanoi. It is sometimes called the Mountain Campus. The college supplies graduates to the educational sector in the northern mountain provinces, contributing to a gradual narrowing of cultural and economic gaps between the customarily primitive and poor people from this mountainous region, and the richer, more educated people from the lowland areas.

I can relate to this mountain concept and philosophy of educating the mountain minorities. My own university, Northern Arizona University in Flagstaff, Arizona, located in the midst of the world's largest ponderosa pine forest at the base of the tallest mountains in Arizona, the San Francisco Peaks, is often referred to as "the mountain campus." One of NAU's charges is to recruit and educate as many Native Americans as possible. The educated students from the Navajo, (the largest Native American tribe;) the

97

Hopi; and the Apache Nations are encouraged to return to their reservations to assist their tribal members in schools, hospitals, businesses, and social agencies. This is a challenge to our university and very necessary for our Native American population.

I learned that Viet Bac Teacher Training College's biggest mission is to educate the ethnic minorities of the mountainous areas of Vietnam and to encourage as well as entice them to go back to their villages to assist the people for life's challenges. One of the college's major goals is to erradicate illiteracy among the minority tribes, following the Ministry of Education's mandate for the entire country. NAU and VBTTC are similar in many respects and worlds apart in others.

The trip leaving Hanoi was again a nightmare, only because I believed that we would surely be involved with any number of fatalities involving cyclos, bicycles, and motorcycles, who headed straight toward us in great waves of humanity, as we sped out of the city limits, crossing the Red River, bound for Ha Bac Province.

Accompanying Linda and me, was my interpreter for this assignment, Mrs. Vu Thi Quy, of the International Relations Office of Hanoi National Pedagogic University. She was educated in English at Canberra University in Australia. We shared with her the day's news that we had heard on "Voice of America" radio earlier that morning. Before long, we were completely engrossed in seeing the sights of village after village, as we progressed on our journey. Again, we enjoyed seeing the beautiful fertile fields of rice paddies being planted. I still feel the women of Vietnam, young and old, work too long and too hard. I felt sorry for them, as I observed them carrying by shoulder yokes heavily laden buckets full of hundreds of rice sprouts encased in thick coverings of wet mud. It really is back-breaking work. My own daughters in Arizona might not feel so exhausted from their office duties if they could witness these typical pastoral scenes. The rural women of Vietnam do not have it easy in any phase of their lives.

We passed several military cemeteries which are always sad for me. Every time I see one, American or Vietnamese, I always think of the poignant words of the once-popular, anti-war tune of the sixties, "Long Time, Passing." There was even a funeral procession with all the mourners dressed in their traditional white and playing music from the back of a truck.

After about two hours we finally reached the Viet Bac Teacher Training College on Luong Ngoc Quyen Road in Thai Nguyen City of Bac Thai Province. We were met by the Rector of the college, Dr. Nguyen Duy Luong. He introduced me to his assistant, Ha Cat Du. As we were led into a reception room on the second floor of the administrative building, we passed faculty and staff members having a morning break of the traditional noodles and tea. In the reception room we were offered the now familiar Coca Cola in cans imported from Singapore, and crackers that I expected to taste like Ritz but actually had only the round size and shape but tasted somewhat sweet. Of course, there were orange slices and hot tea. The room itself was very nice with comfortable furniture arranged somewhat like that of a physician's waiting room. After introductions all around and polite talk, I presented Dr. Duy Luong with an official NAU lapel pin, and NAU Shaeffer pen, and a folder with NAU publicity brochures. I likewise gave the assistant, Cat Du an NAU folder and NAU pen. The interpreter and driver also received NAU mementoes. Dr. Duy Luong then bestowed upon Linda and me each a very colorful hand-woven shoulder bag, a craft product of the minority hill tribes. We were most honored to receive them, and even more so when we witnessed the reaction of the interpreter when she also was presented one. Dr. Duy Luong and I then went into formal discussion of universal problems of education. He quizzed me at length about curriculum construction at my university. We discussed mutual problems of education and how they can be solved. We analyzed solutions for funding. He could not believe the concept of corporate giving for public education. He was fascinated by this and did not tire of my many examples at NAU. He asked me about class scheduling, degree plans, requirements for graduation, available degrees, professorships, and extended education,. He explained that due to the goal of education for the masses, new schools are constantly being built and almost immediately being expanded with additional classrooms. He also said that western curriculum has been introduced, and English is now being taught in all schools, replacing Russian; however, Vietnamese and French are still offered. In spite of the increased demand, there is a shortage of qualified teachers and students are not going into the teaching field due to the low pay and low social status. Lack of funding for education seems to be a universal problem.

Dr. Luong was anxious to show us the computer center and laboratory. We walked across a spacious dirt courtyard into a building in much need of paint and repair. Even the stairs were rickety. The computer lab was housed in a dreary, dark, dilapidated room. The school was only founded twenty-eight years ago, in 1966. It looked like something from the US in 1936, with no upkeep having been done in all that time. There were six computers lined up on one side of the room, eight computers in the main room, three computers in the teacher's section, and four computers in a tiny side room. I looked for and only saw one printer. They proudly boasted that these Japanese computers came from Canada. They also said that these twenty-one computers had to serve 400 teachers and cadre, twenty-five-hundred students, and faculties for linguistics, history, geography, literature, citizenship, education, biology, chemistry, and foreign languages of English and Russian. If they can actually handle all those needs, they do extremely well with very little. I did not hear any complaints nor disgruntlement. They obviously would like to expand, and they need help. They allowed me to photograph the rooms and equipment. Then we returned to the reception room for more round-table discussion. I was introduced to a young Vietnamese faculty member who teaches English and was educated in Moscow. She spoke English with a Russian accent. After more

Coca Cola, tea, and oranges, Linda and I both were dying to use the facilities. We were led to the end of the building and a padlock was removed from the door as we were motioned to enter. We looked at each other, shrugged our shoulders, and filed in. Linda went right, and I went left. It was a medium-size room separated in the middle with a six-foot tile wall. My side revealed an open tile trough in which to urinate and a bench-like toilet. Linda's side was the slit-opening in the floor which must be straddled. Interesting.

We were then told that we were invited to a lunch at a local hotel in Thai Nguyen City. We all boarded three different automobiles and were driven through dusty, winding, and hilly streets into a large cobblestone courtyard. The hotel was built by and for Russians, who occupied the entire building all during the "American War," as the Vietnamese referred to this conflict. It appeared to be under renovation, but I was told this was the permanent status. There was no money for repairs. The Russians were gone, and they left the hotel in poor condition. The tile on the floors was loose or broken, many windows needed to be replaced, the cement walls were cracked and flaking, many electrical fixtures were broken, the curtains and drapes were torn and dirty, and the furniture was shabby. The entire building needed painting; however, before that, something needed to be done to eliminate the mildew from the walls. (This seemed to be a problem of the majority of buildings I had seen in Hanoi. In fact, Roy and Delores have several large dehumidifiers in their home, which need to be emptied at least twice a day.)

We were led into a private room that was partitioned from the main dining area by a large portable screen. There was a long rickety table with some shaky wooden chairs on which to sit. Fresh flowers centered on a white tablecloth spread over the table with matching white cloth napkins at each setting was an attempt at elegance. Immediately a tray of Coca Cola in cans and cans of Ba Ba Ba Bier were placed in front of us. I was encouraged to try the Vietnamese Ba Ba Ba Bier by the seven faculty members in attendance. Our first course consisted of delicious hot vegetable soup with a large freshly baked French roll. Next, came several plates of large chunks of meat accompanied by crisp and hot French fries. (I suspected that the meat was dog meat, which is very popular, especially for men, in many areas of Vietnam.) I ate several pieces, and it did not taste like anything I'd ever eaten. (By then, I was convinced it was dog.) Then we were served generous bowls of the famous homegrown Vietnamese rice with a different kind of meat. (Now, I'm positive the first was dog meat.) For dessert, there was the usual fruit, which we always enjoyed. I really do not need ice cream, pie, nor cake for dessert for every meal, but it's hard to resist. Their tangelos were tart and juicy and much healthier for me than some high-fat, calorie-ridden concoction.

Just prior to leaving the dining area, we heard many firecrackers exploding and thought that people were still having a post-Tet celebration. However, upon returning to our car, we noticed a bridal couple emerging from their decorated automobile, about to enter the hotel. I quickly took photographs and then smiling, clasped my hands in a good-luck gesture toward them. They returned the smiles and bowed to me, another Vietnamese vignette that I will cherish.

Upon our return to the campus after lunch, I insisted on visiting the dormitories. The majority of students were just returning from the Tet holiday. Bamboo mats as well as clothing and bedding fluttered from the window sills of the four floors of the dorms. The airing-out was necessary due to the high humidity and the heavily populated quarters. We learned that eight students were assigned to a room, and that two rooms shared a bathroom. It was definitely not the new American university style with two students per room, private bath, telephone, TV, stereo, computer, fax, refrigerator, microwave, tape recorder, etc. This was dormitory living in the most primitive sense, roughing it 100 per-cent. The students looked like the everyday teenager: giggly, excited to see friends from whom they'd been parted a week or so, and extremely curious about two Americans observing them "on their turf."

After a short visit to the dorms, Dr. Duy Luong took us back to the reception room for more refreshments and talk about our professional lives. He asked me what my teaching experience was about. I told him I had taught every level from seventh grade through the university level, including high school and community college. He replied he had taught elementary and high school, junior college, technical school, and university. We were quite surprised that our backgrounds were so similar. As we continued to compare our lives, we realized we had much in common: first-born sons, bachelor degrees earned at a mountain campus, military service immediately after high school during wartime as enlisted men and volunteers, thirty-five plus years in education. We each began our careers as junior high school teachers and are now university administrators. We have been honored as teachers. He was named outstanding teacher by his government. I was nominated for Arizona Teacher of the Year and was the recipient of the Freedom Foundation Teacher's Medal. We both pray for peace, good will, trust, and exchanges in education. We are both worried and concerned about funding for education, teacher salaries, campus improvement, and employment for our graduates. Dr. Luong and I found we had more similarities than differences in our lives. We are of a different culture, nationality, religion, citizenship, and socio-economic level, and yet, I still felt a kinship and close relationship to him that is hard to explain. We were almost instant close colleagues. I only knew him for one day, but I felt warm friendship with him. We shook hands warmly and parted reluctantly, not wanting this day to be over. We both sensed that we probably would not speak to each other again, yet, I yearned to continue our professional and personal association.

Just prior to my stepping into the automobile, Dr. Luong patted my shoulder and said, "From one old military man to another, I salute you." He popped a snappy military salute to me. I, in turn, came to attention and raised my right arm in a perfect military salute to him. We remained in this military mode for several seconds before we each smiled and said, "Good bye." When Linda and I were chauffered off, I thought, this man's campus needs several million dollars just to get it to a basic functional level. The buildings were in great need of repair. Large stagnant ponds should be checked for malaria breeding grounds. Everything was in need of cleaning and painting. I have never seen an educational institution that needed more "fixing-up" than this one. I feel so sad and sorry for the students, faculty, administration, and staff. The people of Vietnam are so friendly and warm to us. The war is the worst catastrophe that could have happened to them. They have suffered terribly. I do not see them fully recovered in fifty more years. I pray I am wrong. I thank God I am an employee in a modern, beautiful, progressive university. NAU is "wealthy" in comparison.

We were driven back to Hanoi, again facing mega traffic, experienced only in Vietnam. There are no traffic signs, traffic lights, nor speed limits. "Anything goes" in driving. Whoever reaches the intersection first has the right of way. Just honk your horn or ring your bell and proceed full speed ahead. You may pass traffic on either the left or right, whichever is more convenient. It is chaos to us, but standard operating procedure to the Vietnamese.

Upon arriving back at the Morey's, we showered and waited for Roy to return from UNDP headquarters so we all could drive to Loan's home for dinner. Tonight we were to have the rare privilege of visiting a Vietnamese family for a home cooked meal. As the official UNDP automobile drove into the courtyard of the complex built for government workers, we were met by Loan's husband. He greeted us and led us into the building. Curious neighbors left their own apartments and closely watched every move, as we four Americans climbed the stairs to the second floor. Everyone smiled and seemed pleased that we were there. Loan welcomed us and introduced us to their eleven year old son who looked as if he were about eight. He was a very polite, well mannered boy, but more interested in an evening of watching satellite television from Hong Kong, than in making small talk with foreigners. Their eighteen year old daughter who looked as if she were twelve, was presented to us. Less than five feet tall, slender, and absolutely beautiful, she was also very skilled in the culinary arts. Before dinner we were given a tour of their living quarters. Loan and her husband proudly showed us the newly installed sliding windows in their bedroom. Surprisingly, each of the children had their own tiny bedroom. The small living room contained that ever-present TV set, a large picture of Ho Chi Minh, and family photographs. They had erected a large screen room divider to section off a portion of the living room as a dining area. The kitchen was extremely small but must have been functional, proven by the delicious meal prepared there for us. Loan and her husband asked us to sit in the living room and have the traditional green tea in small cups. Next, we were going to be treated to a glass of champagne, to toast the event. Loan was quite excited as her husband was attempting to pop the cork from the bottle. Her exhilaration turned to dismay as she saw there was no sign of carbonation. Champagne without bubbly meant something was wrong. Roy looked at the bottle, discovered it was Russian and sadly declared it had gone bad. Delores saved the situation by insisting they open the bottle of California wine she had brought as a hostess gift. The dignity of the occasion was restored.

Soon after the toast, Loan and her daughter began to serve the lovely eleven course dinner, prepared almost completely by the charming eighteen year old. I could not imagine the average American high school senior, after having been in class most of the day, coming home and preparing such a meal for guests, because her mother worked outside the home all day. We were impressed not only with the effort but also with the expertise and graciousness. There were rice, noodles, soup, tofu, chicken, beef, fish, vegetables, fruit, potatoes, and yams. We were even given a choice of Ba Ba Ba, Carling Ale, Seven-Up, Coca Cola, or Canada Dry to drink. For dessert there was papaya and custard apple, after which we retired to the living room and were served lotus tea, fresh mulberries and sponge cake. It was a sumptuous and tasty meal, and we bestowed many compliments upon the chef.

Conversation was limited because Loan's husband did not speak much English, so everything had to be translated to and from him. He was an important government official and full member of the party with mid-bureacratic rank. He had been assigned this apartment for a very nominal rent and a government car picked him up every morning and brought him home every evening. These were the perks of his position.

Upon leaving, we warmly thanked Loan and her spouse for their generous hospitality, and I presented both children with an NAU pen and pencil. Driving back through nighttime Hanoi was interesting. There was an absence of street lights and very few neon signs. The still-open stores were dimly lit. The streets were still crowded with ringing bicycles, roaring motorcycles, and jingling cyclos. The reflection of the soft lights in the Lake of the Restored Sword was lovely and must have been enjoyed by the stream of young lovers strolling along its banks.

It had been a long day and there was no need for a night cap tonight. We willingly went off to our bedrooms. As Linda and I got ready for bed, we looked at each other and I grinned that smile of contentment and wonder. We were touched and felt so honored for having been invited into a Vietnamese home to share their evening meal.

Dr. Hguyen Duy Luong, Mrs. Vu Thi Quy and Chuck

Viet Bac Teacher Training College

Dormitory of Viet Bac Teacher Training College

Loan and Spouse opening champagne

# Chapter Seven

# UNCLE HO

Today was the day we were finally going to be taken to visit the Ho Chi Minh Mausoleum. After our customary breakfast of papaya, toasted French bread, and coffee while listening to the Voice of America, Delores' driver and Loan greeted Linda and me. They were prepared to take us on a private tour of the mausoleum. We drove to the boulevard in front of the monument but were stopped by barricades from traveling closer. We saw an army guard giving instructions to hundreds of people lined up single file, waiting to enter the tomb. Loan asked us to wait in the car with the driver while she talked to an army guard. The guard then motioned the driver to drive around the barricade and park near the sentry station. The guard approached us and saluted me in a military manner. I returned his salute. He asked me for my camera. He then instructed Loan to march behind him and instructed Linda to march behind me. As the guard and I strutted shoulder to shoulder past the long lines of patiently waiting visitors, I felt somewhat guilty but relieved that we didn't need to go to the end of that line. We four marched down the middle of the boulevard, did a left face and climbed up the three sets of stairs. At this point the guard inspected us. I later learned that all collars must be down, buttons buttoned, and hands out of pockets.

He then asked us to follow him. We went through the doorway into the massive structure itself, down a hallway, and then turned into the actual room where President Ho Chi Minh lies in state on a raised catafalque, slightly angled so that visitors will get a complete view of him as they slowly walk the perimeter of the glass casket.

The bier on which it rested was just below eye level in a large dark pit, so it almost appeared to float in space. At each corner of the room four army guards in crisply starched uniforms, stood at attention with rifles and fixed bayonets. We were not encouraged to linger. We finished viewing "Uncle Ho" and exited through a doorway into a hallway and out the opposite side of the mausoleum structure. As we stepped up our pace and reached the parade viewing area, the guard handed my camera back to me. I asked him if I could take his picture, (in sign language.) He abruptly answered an unquestionable "No." I then asked if I could photograph the monument with the overly large Vietnamese flag flying above it. He agreed, so I was able to get a picture of the mausoleum, the Vietnamese flag, and the guard too. It is a very solemn experience to be led through the tomb.

Ho Chi Minh is revered as a demigod by the Vietnamese, particularly in Hanoi. Loan explained to us the importance, reverence for, and stature of Ho Chi Minh. She then guided us down a beautifully manicured path around a small immaculate lake filled with carp to President Ho Chi Minh's residence. My preconceived ideas of a large palace style structure were completely erroneous, as we

114

viewed a rather small bungalow on stilts. The whole building was smaller than an American two-bedroom tract home. The downstairs area was a large open room encircled with a bench where conferences and meetings had been held. Stairs at each end led to the private living quarters. The entire structure was made of beautiful dark wood, and shutters were used to enclose the rooms for privacy and protection from bad weather. Glass has been installed so that the shutters can remain open for visitors to view the inside of this quaint domicile. We walked around the residence and climbed the stairs and were able to see Uncle Ho's desk, books, bed, hat, jacket, notebooks, pens, cane, walking sick, and gifts. The small structure is simple in design. It is very plain and almost austere. There are no frills nor surplus furniture. I saw one lamp and no easy chairs nor sofas. Ho Chi Minh lived a simple life, and it was certainly reflected in his residence. There is a railing in front of his study, where, according to Loan, children were invited to come and speak to him. She also related that Ho Chi Minh walked out of his home, just steps away from the shore of the large pond and sounded a signal to the carp to come to him so he might feed them. Within the residence there was a path which led directly to an underground bomb shelter. Outside the shelter we could see a large artillery shell suspended from a cross bar. During the war the president was warned of air attacks when the shell was struck with a hammer, but now it is only a tourist curiosity. Beautiful flower gardens surrounded the residence, and lined all the pathways in this park like setting.

115

I took photos of the residence inside and out, then walked on a path leading to the Presidential Palace, adjacent to the residence. This impressive structure is presently used for receiving international envoys and holding state receptions. Loan told us that when he assumed his UN post in Hanoi, Roy was received by the government at the Presidential Palace. I teased Loan that I was hurt that the Vietnamese government did not receive me here. She is not in tune to American Chuck's humor and just looked at me very puzzled. I said, "Only joke, Loan, only joke."

The grounds of the Ho Chi Minh Mausoleum, Ho Chi Minh Residence, Presidential Palace, and museum of Ho Chi Minh comprise over a square mile of land area in downtown Hanoi. All of the general area is lushly and beautifully landscaped. It is in sharp contrast to many other locations of Hanoi that are dirty, dingy, falling down, in disrepair, and in need of paint.

Down another pathway I could not resist a souvenir stand, where I purchased an olive drab colored Vietnamese pith helmet. Immediately, I thought of my brother Morrie and my two grandsons Chase and Collin, so I bought three more helmets. This time I chose red, white, and blue ones. Loan bargained for me to make sure I got the lowest prices for all my souvenirs. Being able to help us bridge the cultural gap, she was an invaluable friend in so many ways.

Loan directed the driver to return to the Morey residence by way of the Center of Cultural-Scientific Activities, the oldest university in Vietnam. It was interesting to see it again. Back at the

Morey's, Delores asked us if we'd like to accompany her as she delivered the Hanoi International Women's Club newsletter to various embassies. I jumped at the opportunity for another great photo session in Hanoi. We stopped briefly at the embassies of Indonesia, the United Kingdom, Canada, Australia, New Zealand, Japan, Germany, Cuba, China, France, and Italy, as Delores completed her rounds. We ended up our "tour" with a visit to an art center, where several ladies in the organization were taking a class. I took the opportunity to view and photograph the crumbling war time sculpture placed in the courtyard. These statues depicted men, women, and teen soldiers in various forms of combat. There were women with rifles and field artillery; soldiers in attacking stances with bayonet mounted rifles; wounded and dying soldiers; and soldiers of both genders carrying flags into battle. Linda wasn't even interested enough to get out of the car to see them, much less photograph me with the sculptures.

Delores returned and asked the driver to take us to "Silver Street", where Linda and I purchased several pieces of handcrafted silver: small boxes and bottles of many shapes, miniature animals, and figures depicting various lifestyles of the Vietnamese people. We were quite charmed by all the antique furniture we saw. Our daugher-in-law Liz would have been enchanted. Afterwards we went to a few shops close by and found several tee shirts embroidered "HA NOI", some silk kimonos, and some children's clothing, which we snapped right up. I even purchased a tee shirt for myself.

117

While driving home, we suddenly spotted a large crowd in front of an impressive French style building. I was informed that the building was the Vietnam Supreme Court. Hundreds of people were milling about in front of the building, overflowing the sidewalks and filling the streets. Traffic was stalled by the crowd, awaiting the sentencing of several government ministers and deputy ministers, who had been found guilty of fraud and the embezzlement of large sums of money from a much-needed project in the countryside. (They were eventually fined and sentenced to prison.)

Delores then asked the driver to stop at 202, a Hanoi restaurant where we were meeting Roy for lunch. It was a French restaurant that came highly recommended to us. We started off with Ba Ba Ba Beer. We continued with onion soup, stuffed crab, chicken shish-ke-bob, fried noodles, French fried potatoes, and for dessert bananas flambe. Our table was on a small balcony overlooking a busy Hanoi street. I had a perfect view of the scurrying pedestrians dodging bicycles, bicycles dodging automobiles, cyclos dodging Russian made army jeeps, and vendors hawking their wares. The meal was as good if not better than that of the Lotus Restaurant. We photographed the surroundings inside and out. Our Vietnamese waitress, dressed in her native ao dai, was stunning.

After a delicious lunch, Roy returned to his office at UNDP, and Delores thought Linda and I should get the true flavor of the day, so she arranged for cyclos to deliver us from the 202 Restaurant to her residence. The cyclo drivers, with Linda in one cyclo, and I in another, peddled quickly, dodging cars, bicycles, people, and motorcycles. I think they were bent on giving these Americans the ride of their lives and scaring the living hell out of us. Delores and her driver arrived just ahead of us, and the driver ran into the street to direct the cyclos to the residence. I stepped out of the cyclo smiling and laughing, but secretly thanking God for our safe return.

We decided to walk around the Lake of the Restored Sword. We managed a few stares from the strollers and were urged to purchase items from all the street vendors. We walked into a department store two blocks from the lake, went through a government antique store and perused the art works of a large art gallery. We were constantly besieged by old women begging, begging children, and young boys beseeching us to buy packets of colored post cards. Their plea was always, "Ma-dame`, buy! Ma-dame`, buy?" It was very sad and very pathetic. We had been instructed to refrain from giving any money whatsoever to any beggar. I violated this advice once, when I gave all my coins and Vietnamese bills to a man without arms and legs, propped up on the sidewalk. Something in my heart and soul told me this man was a war veteran. I truly believe he was. I stopped and emptied my pockets into his cup and gave him a half-hearted salute. He does not have veteran's benefits. I felt so sad for him. Damn the wars.

We then strolled to the Hotel Sofitel Metropole Hanoi. The pastel carpeted lobby with its polished brass railings and etched glass windows lent an updated touch of elegance to the fine old hotel. In the pastry shop of Le Beaulieu Restaurant at the Metropole, we purchased a French lemon tart previously ordered by Linda. We walked back to the residence where, to my surprise, Delores had arranged for me to receive my third body massage. I very eagerly hurried up the stairs, stripped down to my shorts, jumped on the bed, and waited for the Vietnamese lady to begin. I was totally relaxed and ready to be jettisoned into a state of euphoria. This was instant pleasure. (I inquired about this same massage when I returned to Phoenix and learned that it was possible to receive somewhat of a body massage at a resort for $75.00 for twenty minutes.)

To accompany a scrumptious dinner, Roy opened a fine bottle of champagne. The dinner was just a tiny bit rushed, as Roy and Delores had a surprise for us this evening. After dinner we were driven to the Vietnam Water Puppetry Theatre on 32 Truon Chinh Street, to view the Vietnam Water Puppet show. I learned that water puppetry is a traditional performing art of Vietnam dating back to 1121. The mode of using water to activate the puppets and hide the manipulators was splendid. The show was charming and delightful. The water gives life to the figures and becomes a character of the puppet show. A French newspaper wrote, "The puppet figures are manipulated with an unimaginable cleverness. It is like they are commanded by a magical power." Since 1984 Vietnamese water puppet troupes have given successful performances in France, Italy, the Netherlands, Australia, Japan, India, Great Britain, and Sweden. This water puppet show would be a tremendous hit in the USA. Our oldest granddaughters, Taylor and Chelsea, would have enjoyed this very creative and ingenious method of puppetry so very much. Every Tuesday, Thursday, Saturday, and Sunday evening at 7:30P.M., Hanoians and visitors are treated to a unique and fascinating bit of entertainment beginning with the musical prelude and continuing with various acts including the Dragon Dance, Farming Scene, Lion Dance, Boat Racing, Fishing, Buffalo Fighting, and the Four Mythical Animals Dance. If by some rare chance, one would not be charmed by the puppet performance, just to view the lovely Vietnamese young ladies singing with and playing in the accompanying orchestra is worth the price of admission.

We passed the Vietnam Air Museum on our way back to the residence, and the silhouettes and shadows of all the Migs and helicopters were an eerie sight as we drove along the fence line.

Upon our arrival at the residence, I dashed upstairs to use the rest room. After taking my time and strolling downstairs, I found Linda, Roy, and Delores congregating around the kitchen table with a fancy French cake, (from the Hotel Metropole), placed in the middle of the table. An assortment of balloons with, "Happy Birthday Sweetheart," emblazoned on them, floated above a pile of wrapped birthday gifts. Delores had decorated the cake with permanent sparkling candles. After unsuccessfully trying to blow them out, I received a serenade of the traditional, "Happy Birthday" song. Delores prepared a fancy French coffee, and I unwrapped the presents Roy and Delores had presented to me. First, I opened an exquisite hand-crafted silver box, which I can use to hold stamps or paper clips.   Next was a hand-carved water puppet, a delightful reminder of this evening's entertainment.   Then I opened a dark wood holder for a silver pipe that Roy and Delores had brought to me on their first home leave from Hanoi to Arizona.   It was a wonderful evening with dear and special friends, and a certain reminder that I was one more year older, one more year wiser, one more year well-travelled, and one more year better educated.   It was a fitting day and evening to the celebration of my birth.   I missed my children and grandchildren tonight.

Presidential Palace - Hanoi, Vietnam

"Uncle Ho's" House

Ho Chi Minh Mausoleum

Opera House, Hanoi, Vietnam

科甲申來名不朽

Stone tablets erected between 1484 and 1780 list names of 1306 doctor laureates
at The Temple of Literature and National University
Formerly Oldest University in Hanoi, Currently cultural center

# Chapter Eight

# GOOD MORNING, VIETNAM

Today is 23-February, my birthday. It is thousands and thousands of miles away from Durango, Colorado, my birthplace. It is also my day of departure from Hanoi. The travel schedule now directed me to Ho Chi Minh City. I savored the familiar and last Hanoi breakfast we had with Roy and Delores as we listened to another broadcast of Voice of America on their short wave radio. Delores' driver came to the house to pick us up and drive us to the airport, so we could catch a Vietnam Air flight from Hanoi to Ho Chi Minh City. It is a ride of over one hour from downtown to the Hanoi International Airport. We bade Delores' housekeeper farewell. Saying goodbye to Lap was difficult. She was still mourning her husband's death. Just a few weeks before our arrival, her husband had been one of the many motorcycle fatalities caused by the horrendous traffic in the Hanoi area. I felt so sorry for Lap. She misses her husband.

Delores will not accompany us to the airport because security allows only passengers in the waiting room. After such an impressive visit in Hanoi, saying goodbye to both Roy and Delores was somewhat emotional. We had shared some incredible experiences this past week; however, the remaining part of my mission in Vietnam was to be in Ho Chi Minh City. Roy had contacted his liaison officer, and director of the UNDP office in Ho Chi Minh City, who would meet us at the airport and assist with my official meetings. As we drove through the gate of the residence, I wondered when and if we would return, so I could complete my projected mission.

Once again we faced and braced the onslaught of mass humanity on bicycles, motorcycles, and cyclos. It seemed as if all Hanoi had come out this Wednesday morning to bid us some kind of farewell. As we drove through the city, the driver slowed for the pedestrians at the corner. I was eager to fill my eyes and in so doing, expand my memory bank with our last hours in Hanoi. I spotted a barefoot young boy, wearing cotton shorts and a short sleeved plaid shirt with no buttons. He stared and stared at me. I stared back with a smile on my face. We made eye contact with each other, and for a moment I believe we also made heart and soul contact. He began to smile, then slowly raised his right hand and waved at me. I exuberantly waved back to him. He continued waving, and so did I. As the car slowly traveled through traffic and away from this boy at curbside, I turned in my seat and continued to wave through the rear window. The boy took several steps toward the car and raised both hands, waving until we were out of sight of each other. I turned back around, facing the front once more, and completely ignored the comments Linda was making about leaving Hanoi. I was hoping she wouldn't ask any questions, because I had a huge knot in my throat. I'll never see that boy again or learn what his future holds, but he touched me that day, as we were leaving Hanoi.    The driver pointed out that we were passing the Red River again on famous Vietnam Highway One.  The Red River flows from past the Chinese border in the North through Hanoi territory.  As we continued our trip, we again saw the now familiar sights of rural Vietnam: rice paddies under cultivation, rice being planted, water buffalo tended and driven by young boys, girls busily transporting heavy loads of rice plants to the field, duck herders tending their flocks, boys and girls irrigating the fields by a method hundreds of years old.  We saw the family grave sites in the cultivated fields.  We passed pagodas and Catholic churches, and we saw the hundreds of small entrepreneurs, selling wares of all descriptions.

Upon arriving at the airport, the driver unloaded our bags and guided us to the counter to have our airline tickets validated and our passports and visas checked. He took care of our bags going through security.  As he said goodbye, he wished us well and asked us to return.  He said he never thought he would be asking Americans to return. He had prayed and wished so often that Americans would leave when he was seeking safety and protection during the many war raids that American B-52 bombers made on Hanoi.  He said the present times were much better for all of us. We bade this gracious man farewell, wishing him good health, happiness, and safety always for himself and his family.

We now had over one hour to wait in the waiting room of Hanoi International Airport.  We sat and began to watch the TV set in the waiting room. We grew bored very quickly of the Samsung tv set constantly playing old black and white Three Stooges film clips, followed by old black and white Charlie Chaplin film clips, all in Vietnamese. It was rather humorous, now that I think of it. We moved to different seats, because I grew tired of some obnoxious, portly Australian businessmen, trying to proposition a young Vietnamese girl working behind a souvenir counter. I am glad they were not Americans. Again, we were the only Americans in the waiting room. As we began to queue up for the short bus ride across the tarmac to the plane, I heard German, French, Thai, and Taiwanese language spoken by the passengers. The only English was from Australian, New Zealand, and United Kingdom citizens. We climbed the ramp into the aircraft and were greeted by the French pilot, crew, and the beautiful young Vietnamese airline attendants, dressed in their traditional ao dais. The flight, two hours long, began with another quick glimpse of a squadron of Mig-21s lined up neatly in the military portion of the airfield, ready for whatever. Again it was a reminder of how things must have been "once upon a time." During the trip we passed over the highlands of Vietnam and places that we had heard of or read about, such as Khe Sanh, Hue, Danang, and Pleiku. We were served lunch, but I could only eat the rice and sponge cake and drink the mango juice. The rest of the meal did not look very appetizing.

While on the craft, Linda and I became friendly with our seatmate, Mr. Chuyen D. Uong, Vice President and Resident

Representative for Citibank. He questioned us on my mission, and we questioned him on his position. He was returning to Ho Chi Minh City From New York, to assume the vice president's position for Citibank. Born and raised in Hanoi, he had been a refugee in the U.S., via the Philippines, since 1975. He was educated in the United States, married one of his country's citizens, and is raising their children in New York. His job with Citibank brought him back to Vietnam, while his family remained in the U.S., until he established a home in Ho Chi Minh City. He was very nice and it was interesting learning of his return "home." I could very well become friends with him. We wished each other well in our missions as we left the aircraft.

We landed at Tan Son Nhut Airport after the quick flight. I immediately started pointing out old US military sights, much to the disgust of Linda. Many old concrete oval US Air Force aircraft hangars were plainly visible, and I recognized the US control tower and some former US military buildings surrounded by former US aircraft, jeeps, and trucks. It was a weird and eerie sight to me. Linda almost refused to look or recognize the equipment. We went through the airport ritual of leaving the plane and boarding a very hot, stuffy, and stinky bus that had probably been left by Americans. Some passengers needed baths, deodorant, and a change of clothes. I held my breath, then took a big gulp of air and started the process all over. As we stepped into the airport I spotted a man carrying a sign that said, "Dr. Pilon." We approached and met Nguyen Xuan

Thuan, the Director of the UNDP Liaison Office in Ho Chi Minh City. He had the driver claim our bags and process them through security. We were then escorted out of the terminal, bypassing more security, to a UNDP automobile. We were given a revised itinerary for our stay in Ho Chi Minh City. As we were driven to the downtown area, I noticed a little more order in the driving habits, and I did see some traffic lights and stop signs. I spotted a surprising number of American jeeps, trucks and even several Buicks and Oldsmobiles.

The weather was much warmer and very humid, almost like Bangkok had been. I immediately took off my jacket and wished I were wearing a short sleeve shirt. The city itself looked a little better cared for and certainly more modern than Hanoi. There weren't as many buildings that would require paint jobs. Thuan explained that the hotel where our original reservations had been made was having a water problem, so we were booked into another one, the Saigon Tourist Palace Hotel at 56-64 Nguyen Hue Boulevard. Thuan said he would send a driver and an interpreter to pick us up at 2:00 P.M. so we could have an orientation of the city and sightsee a bit before dinner. He had already personally selected our room, which included a terrace overlooking Nguyen Hue Boulevard. As the driver unloaded our luggage and handed it over to a bell boy from the Palace Hotel, we bade Mr. Thuan goodbye for now and proceeded to check into the hotel.

The small lobby was crowded with overstuffed chairs, inlaid

tables, and floor vases crammed with artificial flowers. It did have a gift shop, which Linda immediately inspected as I checked us into the hotel. The clerk gave me specific instructions not to take all my money nor jewelry as we walked the streets, especially at night because there were many pick pockets just waiting to fleece tourists. Foreigners were the popular target, since they had to carry large sums of American money to pay for lodging, meals, entry fees, souvenirs; in fact everything they wished to purchase. Neither credit cards nor traveler's checks were accepted then, due to the trade embargo by the U.S. We knew this information but did not concern ourselves in Hanoi, because we did not need large amounts of cash any time. In HCMC it was a different story. I cashed a personal check with Delores in Hanoi, and now had over $1000 U.S. in my wallet. I was one nervous customer. As I completed the check-in, I was given a key and breakfast chits for our stay. I turned to pick up some of the luggage and looked around for Linda. The bell-boy quickly grabbed the rest of our bags and asked me if I "wanted girl for room to stay night with you for good time?"

I looked him in the eye and said, "I have girl already for my room," and pointed toward my wife.

He said, "Fine, fine, you have wife. You good man, fine, fine."

We took the elevator up to the room and were very grateful to discover the air conditioning was on in our room. We immediately saw a small safe in the closet, but we never could figure out the combination and refused to ask about it. The large bed had a mattress only about two inches thick and no bedspring, just a platform. All the furnishings: four chairs, a love seat, a coffee table, and the night stands, were bamboo and looked like they'd been installed in the room some fifty years earlier. It would have been like stepping back in time, except for the TV set which broadcast CNN. One adjoining small room contained a bathtub/shower and sink, and another had a toilet and a sink, all very efficient. We opened the drapes and sliding glass doors to a small terrace overlooking the boulevard and observed a working day in downtown HCMC. There were vendors of every description selling their wares, from noodles to postcards. We could see old people, teenagers, and very young children. The younger women were dressed in ao dais. What really broke our hearts were the barefooted children dressed in torn clothing, looking dirty and hungry. Directly across from our room and situated on a median of the very wide street, was a large old French style clock, mounted on a tall post. We could look out the window any time and see the correct HCMC time. We also saw a Fuji film counter and a cyclo station with scores of cyclos jammed together, even blocking the street, waiting for customers.

We unpacked our bags, changed our clothes, and oriented ourselves to our surroundings. Then, we figured out how much money we were willing to take with us and how much to leave hidden some place in the room. After we agreed on this formula, we locked the room and went downstairs. The propositioning bell boy smiled

132

at me and bowed to Linda. Mrs. Huyen, who was to be our interpreter, was waiting for us right outside the Palace Hotel with the car and driver. She was dressed in her lovely pink and white ao dai and appeared to be about eighteen years old. (We later learned she is thirty-one.) She was very soft-spoken and rather reserved on our first meeting. She suggested we drive around the city. I agreed that was a great idea and that we wanted to see it all.

Our first stop was city hall where I took photographs of the statue of Ho Chi Minh, the flags, and all the banners on the buildings. Next we visited Notre Dame, the Catholic cathedral in the center of the city. It was a fine old church, but the interior was dark. There were only a few candles burning and no electric lights. The church was dusty, pews were broken or missing, and the floor needed to be swept and mopped. I stopped and lit several candles in front of the Sacred Heart of Jesus, The Blessed Virgin Mary, and St. Joseph. There were many candles already glowing, the holy water containers were full, and there were many people praying. Mrs. Huyen confided that she was once Buddhist but converted to Catholicism when she married, because her husband is Catholic. She asked me how often we went to Mass and looked startled when I told her we went every Sunday. She said she only attended once or twice a month. As we exited the church, beggars, both children and adults, approached us. Mrs. Huyen warned me not to succumb to them, or I would immediately be surrounded by throngs of them and could even run the risk of being robbed. It was a depressing sight but one we saw on every block in Ho Chi Minh City.

We were then driven to the Presidential Palace, or the Reunification Palace, as it is now called. I found it very interesting that it was on my birthday, 23 February, 1868, that the French made plans and decided to build this palace for Indochina's Governor General in Saigon. In 1954 after the Geneva Agreement, the French were forced to leave Vietnam and turned the palace over to Saigon officials. On 27 February, 1962, two Saigon Air Force pilots bombed part of the palace. Saigon authorities embarked on a new project to make the palace more resplendent. The one hundred room building now comprises a ground floor, three main floors, two mezzanines, and a terrace where helicopters can land. The main entrance is flanked on each side by two "u" shaped wings, which join to become one, directly opposite the entrance and across the large, open courtyard. Lotus pools within the courtyard are clearly visible from the mezzanines above. The furnishings are quite lovely and elegant with beautiful dark, shiny woodwork, and gigantic, exquisite tapestries. This edifice has the ambience of gracious peacefulness.

After the 1962 bombing, it took four years to renovate and refurbish the Palace. It prominently displays the following statement: "Continuing the heroic, long lasting struggles of our ancestors against invasion late last century, and through the two holy resistance wars full of hardships and sacrifices of many generations, culminating with the historic Ho Chi Minh campaign, Vietnamese Army and People have achieved total victory, casting out a new era on our beloved country. At 10:30 on April 30, 1975, the solemn ever-victorious flag of our Fatherland waved high on the Independence Palace roof, tolling the knell of the former regime."

We were very impressed with the design and decor of this splendid palace. Mrs. Huyen had arranged for Linda and me to have a private tour, reserved for foreign government dignitaries. I especially appreciated seeing the military war room, French kitchen, and helicopter landing platform on the third floor terrace. The sloping gardens on the tree covered hill complimented the beautiful palace. It was quite a sight from the top floor, to view the grounds, and in the distance the city. It reminded me of a European city in full glory. Fortunately the Hanoi tank that crashed through the palace gate in the Ho Chi Minh campaign on 30 April 1975, did not penetrate the palace entrance. It was hard to imagine tank tracks through the beautiful lawn and gardens. It is advantageous that the Reunification Palace was saved from destruction and can now be enjoyed by all visitors and can still serve as an official reception center for the Vietnamese government.

At my urging Mrs. Huyen directed the driver to take us to the building of the former American embassy. I was disappointed that this once ultra-modern and sleek center of American activity had been reduced to a run-down building now occupied by a Vietnamese petroleum company. There was some minor construction which consisted of red brick and wood annexes being added to this steel and glass building. There were waist-high weeds where there had once been a lawn. We walked around the building and grounds, asking permission to go to the helicopter pad on the roof where in 1975 Americans and Vietnamese frantically climbed aboard a steady stream of evacuation helicopters trying to "get the hell out of Saigon." Permission was denied. We walked to the front and back doors and fingered the American seal still attached and somewhat defaced. I was told that when the US establishes full diplomatic relations with Vietnam, that by international law, the Vietnamese government will have to return the building back to the U.S. We sure have a large repair bill coming up.

I asked Mrs. Huyen to take us to the former home of General Westmoreland. She said that was easy, and off we went. The villa that he had occupied was well-kept and looked lovely. The general did not live too shabbily, but rather in splendor, such as would be more befitting a head of state. I hope the villa style of living did not distract the general too much, as it was a far cry from the fields and jungles of Vietnam. After driving through HCMC Chinatown, the driver stopped so we could make reservations for my birthday dinner at Roy's suggested restaurant, Piano Bar. After a long afternoon of touring the city, I was grateful to return to the Palace Hotel. It was in a great location, in the heart of the city and in the center of the business, entertainment, and shopping district. We were only seven kilometers from Tan Son Nhut International Airport and within walking distance of Saigon Harbor and Ben Thanh Market.

Upon our return to the hotel, Mrs. Huyen wished us a good,

safe evening and said she'd see us at 7:30 the next morning. Tired and thirsty, we entered our room. Linda asked me to sit down and then presented me with two birthday cards and a small wrapped chocolate heart she had carried all the way from our home in Phoenix. We opened a small loaf of banana bread that Delores had given us when we left Hanoi. (She knew what she was doing by sending something familiar to eat with us.) While Linda sliced the bread, I opened two bottles of Coca Cola from the room refrigerator. We began my birthday celebration with a toast and realized why drinking Coca Cola is "the pause that refreshes." It certainly rejuvenated us.

After changing into fresh clothes, we went to the lobby to negotiate for a hotel car to drive us to the Piano Bar for dinner. I later learned that I was ripped off by the driver for the ride. He wanted $5 U.S., but I negotiated for $4. U.S. We were welcomed into the restaurant very warmly and had our choice of dining in the open garden area or in the closed dining room where the band would perform popular American music of the 40's and 50's. We chose the open, softly lit patio. Being the only Americans in this establishment, we felt pretty conspicuous. We ordered dinner, but only enjoyed the rice, cabbage rolls, and vegetables. The chicken was mostly bones and gristle, very disappointing. To compensate for the terrible chicken, we finished our tea and ordered ice cream sundaes for dessert. They were good. We paid the bill and walked inside for a drink and to enjoy the jazz band music. It felt so odd to be sitting in a HCMC restaurant listening to a Vietnamese jazz band play "In the Mood," "Blue Moon," and "Hold that Tiger." The saxophonist could have played in any American band. He had real talent. After enjoying the music for awhile and getting sleepier by the minute, we asked the cashier to call a metered taxi to take us back to the hotel. The lady taxi driver only charged us $1.40 U.S. I gave her $2.00, and she thanked me over and over.

We watched some CNN World News on the TV and retired to a very hard bed but were grateful for the excellent air conditioning. I guess we were out on the terrace outside our room too long tonight enjoying the night and lights of HCMC, because we had several squadrons of mosquitoes in our room serenading us with their buzzing all night long. If we fell asleep, several mosquitoes would dive bomb us in the most unusual places. Despite the mosquitoes, the ringing of bicycle bells, the honking of car horns, and the yelling of people, we managed to get some sleep. It had been an eventful day in this city with a new name, which had served as a liberty town to US troops for over ten years during the War.

View from our room at the Palace Hotel - Ho Chi Minh City, Vietnam

Helicopter Pad at Reunification Palace - Ho Chi Minh City, Vietnam

Notre Dame - the Catholic Cathedral - Ho Chi Minh City, Vietnam

Ho Chi Minh City street

# Chapter Nine

# CU CHI TUNNELS

I learned that the Director of the UNDP Liaison Office and my host, Mr. Thuan, was actually Dr. Thuan. He earned a Ph.D. in engineering at an eastern European university, following the traditional Vietnamese custom of going abroad for an enriched formal education. Later Thuan was in charge of the North Vietnam news team that filmed the fall of Saigon in 1975, when the South surrendered to the North. This included the tank crashing through the gate of the Presidential Palace, the raising of the North Vietnamese flag over the Palace, and the General of the South Vietnamese Army's formal surrender to the Commanding General of the North Vietnamese Army. Dr. Thuan had arranged for Linda and me to leave Ho Chi Minh City for a day's excursion to the Cambodian border and points between. Our first destination was to the holy see of the Cao Dai religion. When Mrs. Huyen and the driver arrived at the hotel to pick us up, we were quite surprised to see both Vietnamese young people dressed in t-shirts and jeans. It was a complete contrast to the ao dai Mrs. Huyen had worn the previous day.

On the way to the holy see, I asked Mrs. Huyen to show us

any rubber or cashew trees that might be growing in the area. She first pointed out a rubber tree plantation. We could see how the bark of the trees had been scored in a diagonally circular motion. The many coconut, banana, papaya, and mango trees we could easily identify by ourselves. We met very few four wheeled vehicles, but we did see motorcycles busily traveling somewhere, as we passed through dozens of villages. We saw wedding parties, funeral groups dressed in white, and work parties at construction sites. There were rural elementary and secondary schools meeting in open structured classrooms surrounded by large dirt courtyards. We saw more than one group of people who had paid to see a video on a large television screen in a ramada-style bamboo hut.

We saw many Cao Dai temples, as we approached the Temple of Temples, and I tried to recall what I knew of this religion. With a membership of two million peasants and located in the province of Tay Ninh, it is a mixture of Buddhism, Confucianism, Taoism, and Christianity. Some of its saints are Joan of Arc, Sun Yat-Sen, and Victor Hugo. Many people traveling along the roads were pilgrims on their way to its holy see. Directed to park in one of the many large parking lots within the Cao Dai compound, I could not believe the sight before me as we drove through the temple area past the main temple. It was as though we entered a giant panorama of color, or the middle of a rainbow. The ornate temple was quite a sight. It looked like a giant pastel wedding cake, with several smaller versions in close proximity. I got out of the car and was mesmerized by the immensity of the structure and the architectural design.

At the entrance of the primary temple, we were asked to remove our shoes. There was a sign that showed a camera with a cross through it. I asked one of the guides dressed in white if I should leave my camera with my shoes. She said that I would be allowed to take photographs. I was honored. One of the first scenes I noticed was a carved panel depicting the revered multiple deity: Dr. Sun Yat Sen, Victor Hugo, Buddha, Jesus Christ, and Mohammed. We walked down a side aisle to the back of the main altar and up the other aisle. The ornately carved columns portrayed the heavens with the stars, moon, sun, and water. The sights baffled one's mind and created a near kaleidoscope for your eyes. I noticed most of the praying pilgrims followed a Buddhist style, chanting and bowing.

We left the temple and entered the square, where there were hundreds of worshipers who had traveled to make their pilgrimage to this temple. We returned to the car after this technicolor experience and drove deeper into the rural area, passing many large and well-kept military cemeteries. These burial sites honored the "heroes" of the North Vietnamese Army. There are no military cemeteries for members of the South Vietnamese Army.

The driver then asked us if we wanted to see Cambodia. I was not too interested in that venture, but I did say yes. We left the main road and drove through a village congested with people; shopping, selling, going to worship, and milling around the marketplace. After crossing an extremely narrow bridge, we began

143

to see miles of defoliated areas. We were seeing first hand the results of agent orange. It seemed like we drove many miles without seeing anything growing, not even weeds. Eventually, we approached a large concrete building with armed soldiers going in and out. We saw some Caucasians being detained by the soldiers. The men and women were arguing with the soldiers and rapidly losing the argument. I wanted to roll down the car window and yell to them to shut up and get the hell in their cars and leave. The guards informed us that we were not to take photographs and not to even point our cameras nor have them in our hands.

We saw an enormous concrete gate. Higher than the building and above the gate, were six foot high letters of cement, spelling out "Vietnam." Past this massive entry and across a defoliated no man's land of over one hundred yards, was a similar concrete portal with gigantic letters, "Cambodia." We could see armed guards with guns pointed in our direction, and we noted plenty of armament at the Vietnam gate. The driver said that in the daytime, nobody crosses this land, but in darkness many Cambodians sneak into Vietnam, fleeing the Khmer Rouge. Now we understood why that last village had so many transient pedestrians. Most of these people escape Cambodia, sneak across no-man's land, and filter through the barbed wire into Vietnam, traveling this poor road over the narrow bridge into the village. I felt a lot more comfortable and safer when the car was turned around, and we were heading back the 10 kilometers to continue our short journey to Cu Chi, a place I was eager to visit.

The Cu Chi tunnels, located in the district of the same name, were an extensive and elaborate underground network devised by the Viet Cong. This hidden complex literally stretched northwest from the Saigon city limits to the Cambodian border. There were miles and miles of tunnels connecting provinces, districts, and hamlets. They held storage areas, water wells, aid stations, sleeping chambers, kitchens, conference rooms, surgery units, hospitals, and war rooms. Many false tunnels, and booby trap areas awaited enemies trying to penetrate the system. Unfortunately for US troops, the Cu Chi tunnels were built under the divisional headquarters of the US 25th Infantry, "Tropic Lightning" Division from Hawaii. The Americans never knew what kept hitting them. This elaborate, brilliantly planned vast labyrinth was a very successful tactical device that resulted in many Viet Cong victories. The tunnel system had its origin in the 1940's, and since then the tunnels had become the hope for conquering any foreign enemy. The Viet Cong who fought from within the tunnels of Cu Chi were tenacious, often spending weeks or even months underground. The US military, known as "tunnel rats," who ventured into the Cu Chi tunnels after the Viet Cong, were held in high esteem by their commanders and their peers.

As we approached Cu Chi, I observed a very large military cemetery under renovation. Next, I spotted a burned out US personnel carrier and the remains of an American tank. Farther into the area I saw a downed US helicopter. We arrived at the Cu Chi Tunnel area about noon, so I suggested to the interpreter and driver

145

that we have lunch. They knew of a small cafe located on the nearby river. We ordered our meal of the delicious Vietnamese rice, chicken, and vegetables with Coca Cola, which Mrs. Huyen shared with us; however, the driver being Buddhist, sat at our table but had brought his own vegetarian sack lunch. The waitress, a very young, slim Vietnamese girl, was dressed in her customary, graceful ao dai.

Sitting and eating at water's edge, I knew that this river had been well traveled by US gun boats. The dense growth along the stream's banks provided perfect protection for the Viet Cong from the tunnels to successfully attack the river patrols. These river fortresses expended millions of rounds of ammunition, spraying the jungle for the absent Viet Cong soldiers, who would elusively hit and run before the Americans knew what happened. As one American officer said, "They are all around us, but we don't know where they are." I felt very odd when I noticed we were dining in the company of Vietnamese military cadre officers. Their forerunners, enemies of the US, had occupied this entire area some twenty years earlier. There were Vietnamese military installations here that at one time had been a stronghold of American military forces.

I had to use the rest room before we continued on our tour, so I found the public facilities. I started to enter, but a lady stopped me and made me understand it was going to cost me money. It was such an emergency for me that I pulled out a $1 US bill. She laughed and said no and held up some Vietnamese bills. I did not have any small Vietnamese bills, so I offered her American quarters. Again she said

146

no, so I offered her Vietnamese dong. As she repeated the no, I was about to have a very embarrassing accident. Finally Mrs. Huyen approached and explained to the lady how important an American I thought I was and said I had to pee pee. The lady laughed and motioned me into the facility, for free. So now I can brag to all my friends that I got to pee free at the tunnels of Cu Chi.

We were led to a ramada type structure and told to be seated, because before the actual tour of the tunnels we were going to be shown a very important video on a large screen tv. While waiting, I looked to my left and saw a scale model of the Cu Chi Tunnels. I walked up to the glass case. The former Viet Cong soldier noticed my interest and turned on the lights of the display. Now, I thought I knew what the tunnel system was about and how thoroughly elusive the VC were to the US troops. I saw this tunnel plan as an almost impossible web to either infiltrate or destroy. That is why the VC were the victors. I also now understood the American commander's statement, "We are surrounded but the VC are no where in sight."

I then walked from the diorama to my right and recognized an array of weapons on display. I spotted an M-1 Carbine, M-16 rifle, a US military 45 caliber, and AK-47 Chinese assault weapon, and shot guns. They were on display, and I was encouraged to pick them up and handle them. We were the only Americans in the area, and we were being given a private tour by a former Viet Cong tunnel soldier, now a member of the regular army.

The VCR was turned on and we began to see the film on the atrocities inflicted by the "American aggressor forces and the puppet regime" to the Vietnamese people. Film clip after film clip showed US B-52 bombers dropping their multiple tonnage of bombs on cities, villages, country side, bridges, churches, pagodas, and schools. We saw the carnage of villages set ablaze and the civilian inhabitants shot. It was a very effective and well prepared documentary propaganda film that made one stop and think about the stupidity of war, the indiscriminate killing, and the terror of it all. I became particularly nervous and aroused when the documentary showed Viet Cong girls sniper-picking-off US troops in the jungles and rice paddies, who were then proclaimed "American Killer Hero" by their commanders. I lost students and parents of students in that war. I even have a cousin whose name appears  on the Vietnam Memorial in Washington, D.C., but I guess we had our share of "Vietnamese Killer Heroes" named also. As General William Tecumseh Sherman said, "War is hell." No truer words can be spoken.

I was pretty sober when the video ended and pretty shaken when we were led down a trail, past scores of bomb craters. They were marked by little white stakes and labeled "B 52." U.S. aircraft tried desperately to destroy these tunnels, but the carpet bombing technique did not work. It just pock marked many square miles of this land, and the VC lived through it all to fight another day. We were led into the first tunnels and traveled along on our hands and knees into large rooms used as surgical units, headquarters, communications offices, kitchens, sleeping areas, an infirmary, dining area, cooking area, and even a place to entertain troops. There was electricity in the tunnels today, so tours could be taken. I was given a small oil lamp made from a 9MM shell used in the tunnels for light and small cooking. In the kitchen and dining area we were offered some tea and raw manioc to eat. This was the typical diet of the underground VC. I dipped the manioc into crushed peanuts, cinnamon, or crushed cashews. Linda always accuses me of going for the biggest, "If a little is good, more will be better." I chose the biggest piece of manioc, because it looked delicious. I thought it would taste like the sweetened tapioca it becomes. How disappointed I was to taste it in its raw and natural state. It was like the stalk of corn, without the kernels. The diet of the VC left something to be desired.

When we were led into the war room, the Vietnamese soldier took his hat off, placed it on my head, and sat me down at the commander's table for a photograph. It was weird to portray the enemy, but we complied, and Linda snapped the picture. The average VC must have narrow shoulders, because both of my shoulders were bruised and sore when I left the tunnels. My back was a little stiff from bending over. I was told that some VC lived in the tunnels for years.

We continued in and out of tunnel chambers and into false walls, then back out. The VC soldier showed me trap doors, behind which were punji bamboo sticks, sharpened to a deadly point and

149

implanted to penetrate through an infiltrating GI's foot, leg, or groin. I saw traps where a variety of deadly snakes were kept to inflict an instant death on an unsuspecting US hunter. Spider traps, spring traps, and exploding traps were shown to us. There was no way the US could have come out the victor over the Cu Chi Tunnel fighters.

We left the tunnels and continued on the trails surrounded by B-52 bomb craters, burned out tanks, and destroyed weapons. I was led down the trail and asked to locate the entrance to a tunnel. I poked, scraped, stamped, and probed for several minutes. Finally a sack and other jungle debris was removed, and a trap door was opened to reveal five steps leading into the tunnel. I started in but was held back by the soldier and told to look into the darkened hole. The soldier shined his flashlight into the darkness. Below the fifth step was the fatal spot, filled with about a dozen punji sticks, ranging in size from six inches to three feet long, of varying circumferences, all designed to impale the invader, whoever they might be. I took a big gulp and said, "I see what you mean." He laughed, grabbed me by the arm, and led me to the next opening with another deadly snare behind the entrance. The soldier asked me if I wanted to crawl through the escape route in the tunnels to the river bank. We would emerge several hundred yards away, just below the cafe where we had eaten lunch earlier in the day. I declined, feeling I'd had enough of the Cu Chi Tunnels. As we walked back on the jungle trail to the entrance, the soldier asked me if I had been a soldier in the American War. I said no. I had been an airman during the Korean

War. He asked if I were a B-52 pilot. I said no, I wasn't a pilot. I was a staff sergeant and medic in the Air Force. I told him that my job was not to take lives, but to save them. He stood at attention and saluted me. This was the second time I had been saluted in Vietnam. I popped to attention and returned his salute. He shook my hand and said goodbye. He asked me to return.

I wandered over to a structure where I observed more military armament on display. Another soldier came out and motioned me to freely inspect the weapons. The first one I picked up was a US M-16, the basic US infantry weapon in the war. I held it very carefully, inspecting every inch of it. I fingered all the parts and held it to my shoulder in a firing position, taking aim through the sights into the adjacent jungle. The soldier approached me and motioned if I wanted to fire the M-16. I nodded yes very vigorously and smiled broadly. He inserted a clip into the weapon and pointed me toward the jungle, while motioning me to fire. I raised the weapon and began squeezing off round after round. A very strange feeling overcame me as I handed the M-16 back to the soldier and thanked him. I thought this experience was so very ironic. An American was handed a captured US M-16 weapon, that was loaded, and was invited by a former Viet Cong soldier to fire into the jungle. This is a crazy world sometimes. I don't know why I bent down to the ground and picked up two of the empty casings I had just fired. I carried them for the rest of my journey in my pocket, and when I returned to Phoenix, I placed one of them in my jewelry box, and continued to keep the other in my pocket. This is absolutely absurd and silly. I have emptied my pockets dozens and dozens of times, but I still pick up that casing along with my tiny shamrock encrusted pocket knife and replace it in my pocket. Why, I don't know, but I keep doing it. Spooky.

As we drove away from the tunnels of Cu Chi, I asked the driver to stop the car so I could photograph a couple of destroyed US tanks. Linda will not be fond of those pictures. The driver then left the car and walked into the jungle. Mrs. Huyen followed him. At first I thought they were going to relieve themselves, and then I wondered why they would go together. Linda and I don't even do that when we are camping. Then, they both emerged with examples of fruit from the cashew tree. They had spotted some trees and wanted to show us how the cashew grew. A cashew shaped green hull grows outside the fruit. This was very interesting, and we were quite excited to see it. I am easily excited.

Driving toward the village of Tay Ninh I spotted a very large, well kept, and impressive looking North Vietnamese Army cemetery. I asked the driver to stop. Of course, Linda didn't leave the automobile and probably wished I wouldn't be so interested in the military or their cemeteries. I took a photograph of the entrance with the large Vietnam flag, bright fire engine red with a large yellow star in the center, flying from a large flag pole in the center of the cemetery. I walked the length of the burial ground and up and down several of the thousands and thousands of rows of grave sites.

Coincidentally it seemed as though the majority of these men and women died in offensives in 1968. That is the year that I read on the big majority of Military grave markers. All these soldiers are designated heroes by the Vietnamese government. I later learned that while the driver, Mrs. Huyen, and Linda waited in the car, a young man bicycled up and tried to interest them in purchasing a skinned, dressed out dog. Linda, thoroughly distressed, turned her head, while the other two declined the offer. The Vietnamese eat dog meat along with their diet of chicken, duck, and fish. Men often eat dog meat, because it is considered to contibute to virility, and they also believe it is  impressive to women.

We then settled back for the speedy return to Ho Chi Minh City. The driver was slightly lead footed and buzzed us back by 4:00 P.M. He said he would pick us up again at 7:00 P.M. to take us to dinner. We had reservations for dinner at the famous Madame Dai's. Madame Dai is a native Vietnamese, educated in France, and a first rate attorney. Although she is elderly, she still maintains a practice of Law in both Ho Chi Minh City and Hanoi. In former years, when her law practice wasn't so lucrative, she had turned her home and law library into an exclusive restaurant. It was now a very charming and picturesque place to dine. The food was reported to be excellent.

Linda and I took showers, washing off the tunnel dust, and changed clothes, eagerly anticipating the arrival of Dr. Thuan and his wife Mai. We wanted to express our gratitude to Thuan for his courteous hospitality and all the arranging of an outstanding itinerary during our stay in Ho Chi Minh City. Roy and Delores had suggested dinner at Madame Dai's and arranged the reservations for the four of us. At precisely 7:00 P.M. Mr. Thuan arrived at the entrance of the Palace Hotel. Mr. Thuan introduced us to his lovely wife. He sat in the front passenger seat, while Linda and I sat in the back with Thuan's wife, Mai. It was only a short trip to Madame Dai's. We were met by the hostess and escorted to the main dining area in the law library, only capable of seating sixteen people. We were graciously and efficiently served a delicious multiple course dinner that was fulfilling both physically and emotionally. I had to have a Ba Ba Ba beer with my meal. During dinner, we made polite conversation with our new found friends. Just before dessert, Madame Thuan asked me how I liked Vietnam. I honestly related to Mai that I had fallen in love with her country and mentioned how beautiful it is with its tall mountainous highlands, lush fertile green valleys and lovely waterways. Mai then asked me how I liked the Vietnamese people. I told her that the people were very friendly and courteous to me and had gone out of their way to make me feel welcome. I also said that I thought her people were peace loving, religious, and family oriented. I then said that I had come to the conclusion that there was no difference between her and me; that Vietnamese and Americans were the same. I related to her that we are basically the same. We both love our families and worry about our children. We love our countries, churches, and schools. We both dream of the best for all of us. I said that we both laughed, cried,

154

and fretted about our concerns, ideals, and values. We are the same. The only thing that separated us was the Pacific Ocean. As I started to take my first bite of delicious fruit dessert, I noticed Mai discreetly wiping her eyes. Her husband comforted her, and they exchanged a few statements in Vietnamese. Dr. Thuan then told me that his wife was very touched by what I said. She said she did not think that she would ever hear an American make statements like that to her. I touched Mai's arm and told her that I meant every word. More tears flowed, as she gave me the warmest smile I had seen in Vietnam. Dr. Thuan and Mai are both originally from Hanoi and miss their home very much. They are now building a brand new home just on the outskirts of Ho Chi Minh City and are most proud of this undertaking. Mai is personally supervising all the construction and desperately wants Linda and me to return to see their new home someday. I would love the trip back.

After stuffing ourselves with part of our third dessert and enjoying all the antique artifacts placed amid law books on the shelves of Madam Dai's library, I paid the check and we walked out into the night air. We had to wake the driver who was fast asleep in the car. He quickly revived and hurriedly opened all three doors for us. We returned to the Palace Hotel where Dr. Thuan and Mai insisted on getting out of the car to wish us farewell. They each hugged Linda and me good bye. We will not see Mai again. After such a short time of acquaintance we felt we were saying goodbye to a dear and trusted friend. I believe I do have some very good friends back in Ho Chi Minh City.

Linda and I entered our room and sat in our chairs, somewhat mesmerized by the meal, the historic restaurant, and most of all by the great company. The world over, people are basically the same. We are just of different races, nationalities, and religions, but we are all the same race, the human race.

Military cemetery for North Vietnamese Army
located in southern part of reunified Vietnam

Interior of the Temple of Temples - Cao Dai Holy See

Exterior of the Temple of Temples - Cao Dai Holy See

Mrs. Huyen and former North Vietnamese soldier, leading way to Cu Chi Tunnels

Third level down in Cu Chi Tunnel - sampling the mantioc
Chuck, former Viet Cong guerilla fighter (female), Mrs. Huyen, Linda

# Chapter Ten

# HO CHI MINH OPEN UNIVERSITY

I realized the educational system in Vietnam was in a state of flux, due to the upheaval caused by the many wars fought against the Chinese, Japanese, French and Americans. The country has been in a continuous mode of reorganization, adapting and breaking down one system to install another. With the change from one political reign to another, the old cultural and educational machinery became ineffective and deemed harmful to the citizens. Each regime became suspicious of the educational system of the prior administration. After 1955, Vietnamese education under the auspices of the National Government attempted to make decent progress by founding "national educational schools." Due to the country's new independence, Vietnam's current educational leaders maintain it is necessary to use innovative educational methods in bringing up the young to adapt to the current political and cultural paths. I was greeted at Ho Chi Minh Open University by Tran Anh Tuan, Dean of the Faculty of Law. He spoke very good English. When I told him so, he proudly smiled, looked at me with great confidence, and boastfully answered, "Yes, thank you. I am from the Big Orange. I earned and received my Ph.D. at Syracuse University in New York."

He was extremely proud of that fact and enthusiastically announced that he would now take me to meet the President of Ho Chi Minh Open University. We walked into the old building, in need of repair. Waiting in his modest office was Dr. Cao Van Phuong, President of Ho Chi Minh Open University. He did not speak English, but our conversation was facilitated by Ms. Huyen's translation. Dr. Phuong was extremely friendly and hospitable. He told me his university needed much help financially for building repair, books, and equipment. After the formality of introductions and being served tea, we were asked to enter an adjacent conference room, where administrators, department chairmen, and professors were awaiting us for presentation.

President Phuong gave me an overview of his university, H.C.M.O.U. It is open to all students, regardless of academic progress. There are no admission requirements. It is dedicated to the development of self-directed learning and the fostering of in-service training in modern society in Vietnam. Its study programs are for everyone, regardless of age, gender, social background, religion, political persuasion, or nationality. Founded the 15 June, 1990, its current enrollment is 20,000 students. It serves eleven provinces: Can Tho, An Giang, Tien Giang, Cuu Long, Kien Giang, Ninh Thuan, Soc Trang, Song Be, Tay Ninh, Dong Nai, and Phu Yen. A board of directors and academic council assist the president. His administrative offices include academic affairs, finance, logistics, maintenance, and general administration. The four academic departments are social psychology, music and arts, architecture, and women's studies, and the faculties include foreign languages, business administration, computer science, Asian studies, bio-technology, law, journalism, and rural development.

An astounding fact I learned was that the Minister of Education and Training for Vietnam issued the official government decision awarding Dr. Cao Van Thuong the sum of $300 US and directing him to found Ho Chi Minh University, I almost fell out of my seat when I heard this. I could not believe it. After I digested that fact, I have come to the conclusion that Dr. Phuong is a miracle man, who in four short years has attained 20,000 students and eighteen departments at H.C.M.O.U.

We were served the usual tea, Coca Cola, and fruit, but this time there was fresh chilled coconut milk in the husk as well. I began my presentation by bestowing President Phuong with an NAU Shaeffer pen, a lapel pin, and a Northern Arizona University publicity folder. I also gave the attending faculty and administrators NAU pins and pens. After my lengthy address followed by a session of questions and answers, I posed for several photographs with the president. In commemoration of my visit to his university, he then presented to me a very functional black leatherette brief case, engraved with the Ho Chi Minh Open University logo. I am proud to have this memento.

When Dr. Phuong learned that I resided in the city named Phoenix, he told me that the symbol of the university is the Phoenix bird. I explained that there was a large sculpture of a Phoenix bird in the Town and Country Shopping Center near my home. He asked me if I would send him pictures. I said it would be my pleasure.

Dr. Phuong was already committed to some previously scheduled administrative meetings that could not be canceled. Therefore, he asked Dr. Tuan, Dean of the Faculty of Law, to give me a tour of the campus and its classrooms. The first classes I visited were those of the English Department, where I met Dr. Dinh Quang Kim, Dean of the Faculty of Foreign Languages. He spoke perfect English. When I marvelled at this, he proudly beamed, "Why not, I'm an I.U. graduate." Dr. Kim had earned his Ph.D. at Indiana University in Bloomington. I told him that I had attended graduate school at the University of Notre Dame in South Bend, Indiana. He excitedly grabbed my arm and asked," How did Notre Dame do in football this year? I love those Fighting Irish." He was a wonderful character; short, slightly built, with beautiful white hair and the personality of a leprechaun. He asked me to enter one of the classrooms and introduced me to a woman professor from Australia teaching first year English. She was using a very old-fashioned phonograph with "78" records to demonstrate the sound of the language. The odd aspect was that the recording had been done by someone with a strong Southern accent. When I addressed the group, the students were puzzled that I did not sound like the person on the record. I explained that I was from the West. They asked me if I could speak with the dialect of the Southerner. I replied in my

162

usually uninhibited way, "Sho nuff. Yaw wahnt may tuh tawk lahk thi-is?" They roared and wanted more. I reeled off several more heavily exaggerated statements as we took photographs. Several of the students looked at me and said, "U.S., Number one. U.S., Number one."

I visited the second year classes and spoke to them briefly about U.S. education and its English classes. The students were enthusiastic and very pro-American. The courtyard was severely overloaded with bicycles and motorcycles. I don't know how they can tell what belongs to whom. Now, if we could just get American university students to ride bicycles, we could save a lot of acreage from being black-topped parking lots.

Most of the classrooms were small but were overcrowded with students sitting on wooden benches. The chalk boards were the old black ones I had not seen since my own elementary school days. There was only one incandescent bulb hanging from the middle of the ceiling, which gave out a rather dim light. Dr. Tuan, Ms. Huyen, and I walked around the quad, looking into the various classrooms, while making our way to the street in front of the university. Ms. Huyen took several photographs of us shaking hands with the school in the background. Dr. Tuan told me that H.C.M.O.U. is in great need of books, supplies, and money. The majority of their textbooks are plagiarized from decades old US college texts they came by one way or another. I would like to organize a book drive to transport used US textbooks to H.C.M.O.U. The cost for shipping could be expensive.  I would like to talk some publishing company into donating and shipping the books to H.C.M.O.U. free of charge.  The university needs our help.  We Americans did enough to destroy their schools.  Maybe we could now help rebuild them.

Just prior to noon, I was finally able to talk Ms. Huyen and the driver into taking me to the Ho Chi Minh City Exhibition House of Aggression War Crimes Museum.  It is dedicated to depicting the war crimes in Vietnam and begins with a display of the first unit of US Expeditionary force landing in Da Nang on 8 March, 1965.  The guide lectured me and stressed the six million tours of duty that involved US forces.  In 1969, the US military forces in Vietnam numbered 543,000, not counting 70,00 troops from US Allies, plus nearly a million troops of the Saigon "puppet regime."  US aircraft dropped 7,850,000 tons of bombs and sprayed 75,000,000 liters of lethal chemicals on villages, rice fields, and forests in Vietnam.

There is a very extensive but extremely sad display on the 16 March, 1968, massacre at Son My (My Lai), where 504 Vietnamese people were gunned down.  These were men, women, and children of all ages.  I crossed myself and said a prayer for their souls, and the souls of Lt. Calley's men who did this.  Lt. Calley was eventually courtmartialed for this war crime and served a prison sentence in the U.S.

I saw the results of the B-52 carpet bombing raids ordered by President Nixon.  The US. spent $352 billion on the "American War," as it is known in Vietnam.  Tremendous consequences have since been suffered by the Vietnamese people. The results of Agent Orange were shown to me. It was sickening. I saw pictures of the orchards and forests that were heavily damaged by US chemicals. In almost two decades the vegetation is only now barely emerging. Vietnam has suffered horribly from economic, cultural, and social losses.

The museum portrays in very vivid blown-up photographs: the "mopping up" operations by US forces, US soldiers proudly posing with bodies, the molesting and arresting of Vietnamese women, US tanks dragging Viets, the burning of Vietnamese houses, the Binh Duong Massacre in 1970, the dropping of prisoners from helicopters, phosphorous bomb victims, pellet bomb victims, and napalm bomb victims. I saw a tremendous display of various US bombs, tanks, cannon, and aircraft. Linda refused to go. Maybe I shouldn't have either. One enlarged photo was particularly embarrassing to me, as I was accompanied by Ms. Huyen. It was a very large black and white picture of an American GI, probably no older than nineteen, dressed in his jungle fatigues with bandoliers of ammunition across his chest. Smiling proudly, he was posing with six human heads held aloft, three heads in each hand, held by their hair. I silently said a prayer for all seven.

As I was walking into one section from another, I spotted a medium sized frame with a velvet background, covered in glass. I thought I recognized something that was American military. I walked quickly over to the frame, followed closely by Ms. Huyen. She was very curious at my immediate interest. I stood for several minutes staring at the display. My eyes filled with tears, and I was embarrassed for Ms. Huyen to see me. She finally broke the silence and asked, "Do you know these?" I said yes. I pointed out in the middle of the frame, the Silver Star. On each side of it were the Bronze Star and the Purple Heart plus a Commendation Medal. Flanked at each end of this row of medals were the Combat Infantryman's Badge and a Paratrooper Badge. On the upper left corner of the frame, also under glass, was a small bronze plate engraved with

"I was wrong. I am sorry.

Sgt. William Brown,

503rd Infantry."

As I walked away, I also felt sorry. God bless every man and woman, whether American or Vietnamese, who fought in Vietnam.

As I slowly exited the museum, I noticed a souvenir stand and saw the expected; post cards, costume jewelry, watches, Vietnamese Army helmets, reproduced cheap American military insignia, and some authentic US military insignias. As I started to walk away, a very attractive young Vietnamese girl said, "Hey US, you buy these?" she showed me a small cardboard box displaying maybe twenty or thirty US military "dog tags." I picked up some of them, fingered them, read the names, and replaced all of them. Later that evening I thought I should have purchased them all, but then why? I now thought once again of General Sherman's quote, "War is Hell." It really is. We won all the battles but lost the war. Why didn't we learn from the French?

There was very little conversation in the car as we drove away. Ms. Huyen deposited me back at the Palace Hotel, informing me that she would pick me up in two hours for my afternoon appointment. I hurried up the elevator to discuss lunch plans with Linda, once again being grateful of the usual two hour lunch break. Poor Linda had remained in the hotel room all by herself all morning, washing out some clothes, writing post cards, and watching CNN on television with an occasional glance down Nguyen Hue Boulevard to watch the people, traffic and to take in the panoramic view of the city.

Deciding to walk to the Saigon River, we looked for some kind of restaurant or cafe where we could have lunch but didn't find any appropriate place. We finally crossed the street and walked along the river side for quite a way becoming more and more hungry. We then spotted a large, sparkling white structure in the shape of a ship, surrounded by tennis courts, a swimming pool, and a driveway filled with Toyotas. We walked into the dining area of the very plush Saigon Floating Hotel. I told the lovely Vietnamese hostess that we would like lunch. She answered in English and led us to a table. Today they were featuring a lunch buffet with every fruit imaginable, many we had never before seen. It included a complete selection of salads, entrees, desserts, and vegetables. We both ordered from the menu, a Swiss cheese sandwich, which came with French fries and cole slaw, and tonic water as a beverage. For dessert we had ice cream sundaes. The bill was $28.00 U.S. I had paid less than this for a multiple course dinner for four people at Madame Dai's. I almost got indigestion walking back to the Palace Hotel. Mrs. Huyen and the driver asked me where we had eaten lunch. I announced that we ate at the Saigon Floating Hotel. They both burst out in this unexpected Vietnamese laughter. Ms. Huyen said, "Oh no, most expensive place in all city. Never go there, very expensive, too much money." They became interested in what we had to eat and how much we paid. When I told them the contents of our lunch and the price, they again erupted in laughter and said, "Poor people, you spend so much. I can eat for one month for that same US money." I felt very foolish but more educated, for sure.

My afternoon appointment was at Ho Chi Minh City Teacher Training College at 4 Nguyen Trai District 5. I visited with Dr. Do Quang Ninh, the director of the institution and with Duong Tri Duc, deputy director, and their staffs. We exchanged business cards, and I presented them with NAU pens, pins, and folders. It is fortunate that I had been told to bring plenty of business cards, as they are big in Vietnam. It was very warm and humid. Hot tea did not appeal to me that much. I would much rather they would have offered me a Coca Cola, but no such luck today. This meeting was much more low key than the other meetings I had attended or presentations I had made. Perhaps it was the weather. Perhaps it was the language. The people here did not appear too enthusiastic about my walking around their grounds or visiting their classrooms. The discussions were mostly philosophical, concerning general educational practices. The administrators were not too interested in comparative education or exchanging information. I was sorry about that, because the students seemed excited to see me, (due to my being an American,) and all spoke to me, as I returned to the automobile.

When the driver opened the door for me to enter the Palace Hotel, I presented him with an NAU pen and an NAU key chain. As promised I also gave Ms. Huyen two religious medals from the grotto at the University of Notre Dame; one for her, and one for her husband. They inquired if we would like to spend the remainder of the afternoon at the Vietnam Museum of History. I rushed up to our hotel room to ask Linda if she would like to come with us. Linda did not want to spend any more time in the hotel room, so she gladly accepted the invitation. She did ask, however, is there anything on the war? I said no, it is a history museum.

The Historical Museum of Vietnam at Ho Chi Minh City is located at 2 Nguyen Binh Khiem Street. Formerly it was named Musee Blanchard de la Brasse from 1929 to 1956, and then the National Museum of Vietnam at Saigon from 1956 to 1975. At present the museum display consists of two main parts. One shows the history of Vietnam from 300,000 years ago until 1930 and includes the Primitive period, the Hung Vuong period, the period of struggle (1st to 10th centuries), the Ly Dynasty (10th to 13th centuries), the Tvan Dynasty (13th and 14th centuries) the Le Dynasty (15th to 17th centuries), the Tay Son Dynasty (18th and 19th centuries), and the Nguyen Dynasty (19th and 20th centuries). The other exhibits a number of special subjects, bearing the characteristics of the Southern zone, the Oc Eo Culture, the ancient culture of the Mekong Delta, the art of Champa, Ben Nghe Saigon, ethnic elements of the southern provinces of Vietnam, and ancient ceramics of various Asian countries.

I took photographs of the museum building, the Pagoda across the walkway, and of the adjacent Vietnam Zoo. The structures were of fine, old French architecture, and, for once, had been properly maintained to show off this beauty. The grounds had many flower gardens, which were being enjoyed by young Vietnamese lovers, strolling and picnicking. The museum, displaying brightly colored banners celebrating 100 years of existence, was very complete and well organized historically and chronologically. I was impressed and thought any student of Vietnamese history would be pleased with the fascinating displays and accurate information.

After a refreshing drink in our hotel room, Linda and I decided to walk the streets of the downtown area, bordered by Thai Van Lung Street, north to Ham Nghi south, Hai Ba Trmho east, to Nam Ky Khoi Nghia west, to the famous and chic Rex Hotel. We went in and out of shops and walked the entire inside area of the first floor of the Rex. We felt we had stepped back in time as the ambience conveyed the essence of an earlier, more gracious time in Saigon. We made small purchases of bottled water, cashews, and post cards. We stopped at a small book store and bought three children's books for our grandchildren. The total price for the books was $1 U.S. Linda estimated that these same books back home would cost us no less than $12 U.S.

We were constantly besieged on our walk by very young children begging incessantly, "Madame, Madame, please Madame, please Madame." The older children were selling post cards, fans, combs, etc., but also pleading in the same way. I saw many older adults, all very deformed, and many without arms or legs. I suspected in some cases, agent orange, napalm, or gunshot. Toward the end of our tour, a very little girl with nothing on but an oversized, tattered cotton dress with no buttons in the back began following us. She never said a word. As she followed us, she began to hold onto my back pocket or my shirt tail. I stopped and said, "No, please." She just looked at me and held out her hand, palm up. This procedure continued for several blocks. I tried to speed up my walk in order to lose her, but it didn't work. She was the same size as two of my dear grandchildren back in the U.S., namely little darlin' Quin and sweet, lovable Jillian. I became very saddened and actually tuned to Linda once in near tears, and said, "My God, Linda, what is this? What should we do?" We finally crossed a very busy street and the little girl was cut off by the heavy traffic. I didn't see her again, but I see her all the time in my memories.

We bought some French bread back at the hotel restaurant, and Linda and I retired to our room; hot, tired, wringing wet, sadly confused, hungry, and disillusioned. We decided not to leave the comfortable air-conditioned room, so we first rested, and then fixed ourselves a meal of French bread, cashew nuts, dried apricots, tiny bananas, and cool Coca Cola. It was thoroughly enjoyed, though humorously eaten. After dark we ventured out on our terrace, many floors above ground level and looked down Nguyen Hue Boulevard. We could almost see north to the statue of Ho Chi Minh, in the town square, and we imagined the Saigon River to the south. We saw all the begging children in the streets, and we could smell the noodles, vegetables, meats, cooking in the small shops. We could hear the never ceasing hawking of products being sold by street merchants, and the constant ringing of bells from the bicycles and cyclos. There was an abundance of horn honking by automobiles. The Saigon prostitutes were out plying their trade, the muggers were waiting for their victims, and the homeless were looking for an open spot to place their bamboo mats for the duration of the night.

As we stood on the balcony, I looked in the direction of Tan Son Nhut Airport. I remarked to Linda that at times during the war, one could stand on this terrace and see the explosions and fires at the air base. Linda stared at me, turned and walked back into the room, and went to bed. I stayed on the balcony and let my imagination wander to what was in the war years on this street. It was not good.

Chuck being welcomed to H.C.M.O.U.
by Dr. Tran Anh Tuan, Dean of the Faculty of Law

Chuck with Dr. Cao Van Phuong, President of H.C.M.O.U.

Chuck visiting classroom of sophomore English class of H.C.M.O.U.

Chuck meeting with faculty members of Ho Chi Minh Open University

# Chapter Eleven

# FAREWELL, VIETNAM

When we first touched down in Hanoi, I certainly could not imagine that I would have any regrets about leaving Vietnam. I may be the first American to feel melancholy about leaving Vietnam soil. As I looked out the wide terrace window from the Palace Hotel room, I viewed a large panorama of downtown Ho Chi Minh City. The hustle and bustle of the metropolis had begun at daybreak. The prostitutes were off the street. Now was the time for the street urchins, the lame, the private street entrepreneurs, and the ever eager cyclo drivers. The bicycles and motorcycles were out in full force. A generous supply of automobiles, plus a few US jeeps and trucks travelled the streets. Some of the US Army jeeps were painted garish colors. I saw pink, yellow, purple, and red ones. I looked at the large French Colonial style street clock across from our room and noticed it was 7:00 A.M. I thought I would wake Linda for a late breakfast at 8:00. I had packed all my bags the night before, which is my usual routine. Linda was now getting into her routine of packing the morning of departure. We sleepily took the elevator to the fourteenth floor hotel restaurant where we would use our last breakfast chits at the hotel. We had barely stepped into the restaurant when we spotted a familiar face. It was great to see someone we knew, not quite like an old friend, but a new acquaintance. It was Mr, Chuyen D. Uong, vice president of Citibank in Ho Chi Minh City, whom we had met on the flight from Hanoi. We were surprised to see him in our hotel, but he said that he had been bumped to the Palace, as his original hotel had been overbooked. The Palace was very convenient for him, as it was only a couple of blocks to his office.

We asked Mr. Uong to join us for breakfast, and he seemed pleased to be invited. As we began to eat, I noticed that all three of us were having an American style breakfast of fruit, rolls, bacon, and coffee. Linda, Mr. Uong, and I were the only Americans in the restaurant. All the other patrons were Asian and were having noodles, rice, vegetables, and tea. When I mentioned how impressed I had been with Ho Chi Minh Open University, he was very surprised. He said he, himself, had volunteered to teach English to young people, but he felt they just weren't motivated, so he didn't continue it. He also mentioned that his brother and sister-in-law were professors in Hanoi and were grossly underappreciated and underpaid. He said he didn't know how they could make a living. We listened and nodded sympathetically. He told us he is missing his family back in the U.S., and we told him we were sad to be departing this morning. Mr. Uong told us he was sorry to see us leave and that he would have liked for us to visit his office. I had a feeling that if we had stayed longer, we would have had some delightful visits with

Mr. Uong. He spoke excellent English and was both pro American and pro Vietnamese. He was also curious about our opinions of Vietnam and its people.

We were to be picked up at the hotel at 9:50 A.M. I was anxious to pay the hotel bill, because I had nine $100 U.S. bills in my wallet. I was very nervous carrying that kind of cash around on the streets. Neither U.S. credit cards nor U.S. traveler's checks were honored in Vietnam. I peeled out five U.S. one hundred dollar bills to pay for our room and restaurant bill. The change I received was in dong, which I did not want, and some of which I still have. Like the M-16 empty casing from Cu Chi, which I carry in my pocket, I have no explanation why I continue to hang on to these useless items.

Dr. Thuan, the director of the UNDP liaison office in Ho Chi Minh City, and his driver were at the Palace Hotel lobby at precisely 9:50 A.M. We loaded the bags into the trunk and were off for Tan Son Nhut airport. On the way, Dr. Thuan pointed out his new home under construction. We actually spotted Mai, on the top floor of the red brick building, supervising the construction workers, as she had said she must do, when we were having dinner with the Thuans, two evenings ago. Thuan said he hoped that someday we would return, so we could visit his family in his new home. It seemed we had just arrived in Ho Chi Minh City, and now we were travelling the same roads to leave Vietnam. It was over too soon. The driver bypassed the regular security line for automobiles and drove directly to the curb at the terminal. These spots were all by special direction of the guards. Thuan then speeded us to the front of the line where we paid the departure fee of $16 US for the two of us. (I have never understood the departure fee at any airport. It is a rip-off on travelers.) We were then speeded through security at the head of another line, causing some curiosity among other travelers. I felt like a VIP for this action. After checking our bags and processing through a final security check, Dr. Thuan could proceed no farther with us. He stopped to say goodbye. He said we were all set and for us to have a wonderful, safe journey. We told him goodbye and that we felt we had a real friend in Ho Chi Minh City now. We parted, and I found it hard to say goodbye.

It was over an hour before our flight would be departing. Through the plate glass windows, I took photographs of the old USAF hangars, the deserted U.S. control tower, and as many aircraft and buildings as I could spot. I was fascinated to finally see the oval shaped, open ended, concrete aircraft hangars, that I had seen so many times in magazines and on tv. The pre-fabricated buildings were built by the U.S. military, and former U.S. fixed-wing aircraft had been left after the war ended. The diverse group of passengers must have thought I was weird, taking pictures of these subjects, but I continued my photography, nevertheless. The Japanese, Korean, and Australian citizens didn't bother to take any pictures.

Again, we boarded a Vietnam Airlines aircraft with a French flight crew and Vietnamese cabin crew. The ladies were all dressed in their graceful ao dais. We were served another strange box lunch.

I only ate the bread roll, dessert muffin, citrus fruit and warm Coca Cola. As we flew back over Ho Chi Minh City and across the southern provinces of Vietnam on our way to Bangkok, Thailand, I felt so fortunate to have had the great opportunity to make this mission. There are a thousand and one highlights and no regrets. I had a nostalgic feeling as I peered out the window at the last land area of Vietnam we were crossing. My mind was cluttered with thoughts of our Vietnam experience, which soon were replaced by remembrances of home, children, grandchildren, my mom and my brother, the office, my colleagues, and the USA.

Bangkok was not the USA but it was a welcome sight, as we cleared customs and had our passports checked. We merely walked across the Bangkok International Airport terminal covered foot walkway to the Amari Airport Hotel. We checked into Room 3011 and fought with the air conditioning thermostat until the hotel personnel moved us to 4014. The Palace Hotel in Ho Chi Minh City was adequate, but the Amari was plush. We took advantage of all the amenities, walked through the hotel shops, and ate in the restaurants. Everywhere we went, I felt like I had a sign posted on my forehead stating, "I have been in Vietnam." A few people asked us where we were from and where we had been. When I mentioned Vietnam, they all raised their eyebrows and rolled their eyes. We received more of the same when we landed in Taipei.

The United Airline flight from Bangkok to Taipei was far more luxurious than the Vietnam Air, of course; however, the meal was still Oriental. When the attendants asked us how we liked our stay in Bangkok, I answered that we had been to Vietnam. Again we saw the puzzled look asking, "But, why did you go?"

The Chiang Kai Shek International Airport in Taipei, Taiwan, Republic of China, is a far cry from Tan Son Nhut in Ho Chi Minh City. For one thing, the prices in Taipei were much more expensive than in Vietnam. I was not anxious to put our US dollars away and to begin spending ROC en tien. Our tenth floor room at the President's Hotel reminded me of a small hotel in which we had stayed in San Francisco; however, the prices here were much steeper than there. Linda asked me if I was going to buy any souvenirs in Taipei. I told her that everything we purchase in Phoenix is stamped, "Made in Taiwan," so what is the use of packing it all back.

We did arrange to go on a typical three hour sightseeing tour, which included visiting the Grand Hotel, the National Palace Museum, and the Chiang Kai Shek Memorial. Of course, we also stopped at a small shop which sold ROC memorabilia. The clerks and the tour guide were not pleased when we declined to purchase anything. Taipei was very interesting, colorful, and new to us, but somehow it was a let-down after experiencing the sights, sounds, odors, and people of Vietnam. Taiwan is as western as China Town in San Francisco or New York City, only a lot more expensive. Vietnam is Vietnam. Nothing can compare with it. The Vietnamese are happy, loving, peaceful, and hardworking, where the Taiwanese are capitalistic and profiteering.

I am now anxious to get home for my daughter Cheryl's birthday. I was in Vietnam for mine, and I need to be home for Cheryl. I am ready for that fourteen hour flight. While on board the United plane headed for San Francisco, I picked up an in flight magazine that featured an article on the fiftieth anniversary of the D Day invasion at Normandy, France on 6-June-1944. As I read about the U.S. 101st and the U.S. 82nd Airborne Divisions, I got a giant lump in my throat and realized these same divisions bled in both wars.

It was strange to wake up on the first of March in Taipei and land in Phoenix some twenty plus hours later, but still have it be the morning of March 1st. Being driven home from Sky Harbor International Airport in Phoenix by our daughter Cindy, I looked out the window as we approached our neighborhood. I have never seen anything so spacious, green, clean, organized, and beautiful. It was great to be back in the U.S.A. and so good to be home. The first thing our granddaughter Quin said was, "Tell me about Vietnam, Grandpa."

Dr. Thuan, Director of UNDP liaison office in Ho Chi Minh City with Chuck

Farewell to Vietnam at Tan Son Nhut Airport

# EPILOGUE

As I began writing this book, there was no rhyme nor reason to interject anything about the war. I was determined not to make the war any kind of major subject matter. I was made aware by my wife to stay away from the war. This was not a book on the war whatsoever, but everywhere I went in Vietnam and everyone I talked to was involved with the war or was affected by it. Much of what I knew of the war in Vietnam before my mission to Vietnam was through LIFE or TIME magazines. I once had a professor at Northern Arizona University, Dr. Edward Walker, who remarked in class in 1955, "If you can't read, get your information from LIFE. If you can't think for yourself, read TIME." The rest of my sources about Vietnam were the local newspapers and the major broadcasting networks news reports. I definitely had opinions on the war. Initially I believed we were fighting to save Vietnam. As the war progressed, I began to have doubts about the purpose for our being there. One author of the over thirty books I have read about Vietnam said, "We turned all the young women in Vietnam into whores. We turned all the young men into pimps. We turned all the old men and old women into slaves." Another author stated, "We ruined the economy of Vietnam, destroyed the government, amended the culture and religion, and demolished the land." I always supported the American servicemen and women in Vietnam. I am especially touched by the more than 58,000 men and women named on "The Wall." One, Alan

E. Pilon, was a relative. Another, John Godfrey, was the father of three of my students. Paul Loidolt, a student of mine, died of wounds he received in Vietnam, after he returned to the states. His name should also be on "The wall,"

The war was never mentioned nor brought up to me by the Vietnamese people I met. I always initiated discussion of the war or visited the war sites. I became more affected than I could imagine. I prayed, shed tears, and mourned while I visited Vietnam, all because of the war. In addition, I was encouraged by the warm, friendly hospitality shown me by all the Vietnamese people I met. The total experience was very positive, because in spite of my negative rememberance of the war, I discovered a peace-loving people.

The Vietnamese people are far more forgiving than Americans. They respect the United States and look to us for leadership, inspiration, and information. They need our help desperately. They only want peace and unification. They have made this point with the Japanese, Chinese, French, and Americans. They want to be an independent nation in the community of nations, and they want to be a friend of the U.S.A. My wife innocently stated, "The U.S. just got caught up in a family fight." No truer words can be spoken. No one wins in a "family fight." Bitterness remains far too long. We still have repercussions, discussions, arguments, and debates over our own terrible "family fight," the American Civil War. The war between the states was fought to preserve the union.

If I learned anything in my mission, it was that the world is getting smaller, and the community of nations needs to be more friendly and helpful to one another. The Vietnamese are not different from Americans. We are all of one race, the human race. The General of the Army, Douglas Mac Arthur was correct in his message aboard the U.S.S. Missouri in Tokyo Bay, September 2, 1945, when the unconditional surrender of Japan was signed. He stated, "War is the scourge of mankind."

# READINGS

Allen, Richard V. Bartlett, Hall, Colegrove, Kenneth, DEMOCRACY AND COMMUNISM (The Institute of Fiscal and Political Education, Princeton, New Jersey, 1967

Atkinson, Rick, THE LONG GRAY LINE (Pocket Star Books, New York, 1989)

Bleier, Rocky with O'Neil, Terry, FIGHTING BACK (Warner Books, New York, 1975)

Bordewich, Fergus M., "Vietnam: Conquered by Capitalism," READER'S DIGEST (April 1994): pp. 124-128.

Broyles, William Jr., BROTHERS IN ARMS, A JOURNEY FROM WAR TO PEACE (Alfred A. Knopf, New York, 1986)

Caputo, Philip, A RUMOR OF WAR (Holt, Austin, Texas, 1977)

Chanott, David and Toai, Doan Van, PORTRAIT OF THE ENEMY (Random House, New York, 1986)

Day, George E., RETURN WITH HONOR (Champlin Museum Press, Mesa, Arizona, 1989)

Denton Jr., Jeremiah A., with Brandt, Ed, WHEN HELL WAS IN SESSION (Traditional Press, Mobile, Alabama 1982)

Duc, Nguyen Oui, WHERE THE ASHES ARE, THE ODYSSEY OF A VIETNAMESE FAMILY (Addison-Wesley Publishing Company, Roading, Massachusetts, 1994)

Fitzgerald, Frances, FIRE IN THE LAKE (Vintage Books, New York, 1972)

Hayslip, LeLy, CHILD OF WAR, WOMAN OF PEACE
(Doubleday, New York, 1995)

Hayslip, LeLy and Wurts, Jay, WHEN HEAVEN AND EARTH
CHANGED PLACES, A VIETNAMESE WOMAN'S
JOURNEY FROM WAR TO PEACE (A Plume Book, New
York, 1989)

Herbert, Anthony B., SOLDIER (Holt, Rinehart and Winston, New
York, 1973)

Isaacs, Arnold R., WITHOUT HONOR (Vintage Books, New York,
1984)

Karnov, Stanley, VIETNAM; A HISTORY (Viking, New York, 1983)

Kaufman, Marc. "Vietnam Beckons: Come Visit Our Land of Peace,"
THE ARIZONA REPUBLIC: Knight Ridder Tribune
(May 9, 1993,) p.7

MacLear, Michael, THE TEN THOUSAND DAY WAR,
VIETNAM: 1945-1975 (Avon Publishers of Bard Camelot
Discus and Flave Books, New York, 1981)

Manchester, William, AMERICAN CAESAR, DOUGLAS
MACARTHUR 1880-1964 (A Dell Book, New York, 1978)

Mangold, Tom and Penycate, John, THE TUNNELS OF CU CHI
(Random House, New York, 1985)

Marshall, Kathryn, IN THE COMBAT ZONE, AN ORAL
HISTORY OF AMERICAN WOMEN IN VIETNAM (Little,
Brown and Company, Boston. Toronto, 1987)

Marshall, S.L.A., WEST TO CAMBODIA (A Jove Book, 1968)

MacPherson, Myra, LONG TIME PASSING (A Signet Book, New York, 1984)

Mason, Robert, CHICKENHAWK (Penguin Books, New York, 1983)

McConnell, Malcolm, "True Face of the Vietnam Vet," READER'S DIGEST (May 1994): pp. 126-130.

Moore, Harold G., WHEN WE WERE SOLDIERS ONCE... AND YOUNG (Harper Perennial, New York, 1993)

North, Oliver L. and Roth, David, ONE MORE MISSION, OLIVER NORTH RETURNS TO VIETNAM (Zondevan Publishing House, Grand Rapids, Michigan 1993)

Risner, Robinson, THE PASSING OF THE NIGHT (Ballantine Books, New York, 1973)

Santoli, Al, EVERYTHING WE HAD, AN ORAL HISTORY OF THE VIETNAM WAR BY THIRTY-THREE AMERICAN SOLDIERS WHO FOUGHT IT (Ballantine Books, New York, 1981)

Sheehan, Neil, A BRIGHT SHINING LIE, JOHN PAUL VANN AND AMERICA IN VIETNAM (Vintage Books, New York, 1988)

Sheehan, Neil, AFTER THE WAR WAS OVER, HANOI AND SAIGON (Vintage Books, New York, 1991)

Tornquist, David, VIETNAM (The Mallard Press, London, 1991)

Van Zanten, William, DON'T BUNCH UP (Archon, Hamden, Connecticut, 1993)

VIETNAM, A TELEVISION HISTORY, VOLUME I-VII (WGBH Educational Foundation, Boston, 1985 and 1987)

VIETNAM EDUCATION AND HUMAN RESOURCES SECTOR ANALYSIS SYNTHESIS REPORT (UNDP, UNESCO, Giao Duc Vietnam, Hanoi, Vietnam 1992)

VIETNAM TECHNICAL ASSISTANCE IN TRANSITION (UNDP, Hanoi, Vietnam, 1994)

VOLUME I FINAL REPORT, VIETNAM EDUCATION AND HUMAN RESOURCES SECTOR ANALYSIS (Moet Vietnam, UNDP, UNESCO, Hanoi, Vietnam, 1992)

# INDEX

192

Edds, Teall, 25
Fangs, 3
"Fighting Irish", 162
Finland, 58
Flagstaff, Arizona, 4,38,44,91,97
Foreign Economic Relations Department, 43
Freedom Foundation Teacher's Medal, 105
French, 29,35,54,86,92,94,100,128,132,134,135,159,167,170
Geneva, Switzerland, 28,38
Geneva Agreement, 134
Germany, 58,117
Gettysburg Address, 34
Glendale, Arizona, 18
Globe, Arizona, 55
Godfrey, John, 184
GOOD MORNING, VIETNAM, 13,57
Grand Palace, Bangkok, 12, 20
Grand Hotel, 180
Ha Bac Province,98
Hac Pham Minh, 43
"Hallow", 53,88
Ham Nghi, 170
Hanoi,1,3,4,8,14,16,18,24,25,26,27,28,29,46,50,51,62,63,76,79, 85, 89,
        97,102,114,116,117,118,122,124,125,126,127,129,130,131,135,
        137,153,155,175,176
Hanoi Airport, 22,125,127
Hanoi Flag Tower, 53
Hanoi International Women's Club, 117
Hanoi National Pedagogic University, 98
Hao Lo Prison, "Hanoi Hilton", 18,23,29,32,41,42,88
Hawaii, 18,42,145
Hieu, Mr., 72,73,74,75,76,77,84
Historical Museum of Vietnam, 169
Ho Chi Minh, 34,35,50,54,91,114,115,133,134,135,172
Ho Chi Minh City, 1,9,14,47,125,126,129,130,134,139,140,141,153,
        154,155,156,169,175,176,177,178,179,180,182
Ho Chi Minh Mausoleum, 35,47,52,53,85,113,116,123
Ho Chi Minh Museum, 34,40,42,116
Ho Chi Minh Open University, 160,161,163,164,173,174,176
Ho Chi Minh Teacher Training College, 168
"Hold that Tiger", 138
Hong Kong, 9,27,49

# ABOUT THE AUTHOR

Charles Pilon received his Bachelor of Science degree from Arizona State College, (now Northern Arizona University), and taught in the Madison School District in Phoenix for eighteen years. He attended Arizona State University, University of Notre Dame, Lehigh University and the University of Colorado while earning both Master and Doctorate degrees. In addition to teaching, Pilon coached football, basketball, and baseball at Bourgade Catholic High School while also teaching in the evening division at Phoenix College. He was nominated for Arizona Teacher of the Year and has been honored by the Northern Arizona University Alumni Association. In 1988 he was named the Notre Dame Man of the Year in Phoenix. While serving on the City of Phoenix Human Relations Commission, Dr. Pilon was named to Community Leaders and Noteworthy Americans. Having written three textbooks on Arizona and US government, he was named to Who's Who in American Education. Pilon has lectured extensively in Arizona, and in 1992 he had the opportunity to speak in Australia. At the invitation of the United Nations Development Programme, he addressed Beijing Normal University in China as well as several universities in Vietnam. Since 1978, Dr. Pilon has been employed by Northern Arizona University as an administrator of Statewide Academic Programs in the greater Phoenix area.

His wife Linda, a former high school English teacher at Xavier College Preparatory High School in Phoenix, also graduated from Northern Arizona University. Their four children plus spouses: Terrence and Lisbeth Pilon, Carin and Kelly Robinson, Cheryl Pilon, and Cindy and Kelly Mero, have presented them with six grandkids: Chase, Taylor, Chelsea, Jillian, Quin, and Collin.